T0352413

GREEN
WITCHCRAFT
IV

About the Author

Ann Moura has been a practitioner of Green Witchcraft for over fifty years. She holds a bachelor's and a master's degree in history. Moura lives in Florida, where she runs her own metaphysical store, presents public rituals, and teaches classes on the Craft. Visit her online at www.annmourasgarden.com or www.lunasolesoterica.com.

ANN MOURA

GREEN
WITCHCRAFT
IV

WALKING
THE FAERIE PATH

Llewellyn Publications
WOODBURY, MINNESOTA

FIRST EDITION
Second Printing, 2023

Book design by Rebecca Zins
Cover design by Shira Atakpu
Runes on page 153 by Llewellyn Art Department

Llewellyn is a registered trademark of Llewellyn Worldwide Ltd.

Library of Congress Cataloging-In-Publication Data is on file with the Library of Congress

978-0-7387-6427-6

Llewellyn Publications
A Division of Llewellyn Worldwide Ltd.
2143 Wooddale Drive
Woodbury MN 55125-2989

www.llewellyn.com
Printed in the United States of America

Other Books in the Green Witchcraft Series

The Green Witch Tarot
with Kiri Østergaard Leonard

Tarot for the Green Witch

Mansions of the Moon for the Green Witch:
A Complete Book of Lunar Magic

Grimoire for the Green Witch:
A Complete Book of Shadows

Green Magic:
The Sacred Connection to Nature

Green Witchcraft III:
The Manual

Green Witchcraft II

Green Witchcraft:
Folk Magic, Fairy Lore & Herb Craft

contents

Introduction

Please do not skip this introduction. The focus of Faerie in this book is not particularly Celtic nor specific to any cultural tradition. The Other People have been encountered worldwide and each culture supplies its own customs and folklore, much of which is viewed through the spectrum of a localized or otherwise dominant spiritual worldview. My intention in this book is to present the reality of Faerie unencumbered by an external cultural lens or religious interpretation, although there may be some mention of these perspectives in passing. This book is about what I and my students and ritual participants have seen and experienced. I have not written extensively on this subject because it is very personal and there are powerful energies involved in this kind of contact, thus I consider this to be a book better suited for the advanced practitioner.

At age 73, I have been given confirmation that this is the right time to share what I know. I have asked through various modalities and the answer has been consistently yes, do it. Because of this, I believe there is a reason for this information to be put into print for the general public. This book is based on real-life experience and covers real events, real encounters, and even some of the consequences of these. Although more appropriate for the advanced practitioner of the Craft, it is my hope that the details I present will be sufficient for the layperson who is sincerely drawn to Otherworld to make an informed decision as to whether or not to attempt contact.

The book is about fact, not lore, although some people may have difficulty accepting that. As with most unusual phenomenon, it is easier for a person to explain away the strange as a trick of the mind until they actually experience it for themselves. This has been a major reason for my prior reluctance to write about the reality of Faerie and the Other People. For over twenty-five years I have taught many classes on the subject of Faerie and conducted public sabbats, full moon and dark moon esbats, and a number of sidhe moon ("fairy moon," or the second dark moon in the same solar month) esbats for groups of eight to forty-five or more people. During the sidhe moon rituals I have opened portals for the participants to look into Otherworld and possibly connect with a potential companion. This book includes the experiences related to me by some of these participants, as well as those by people who have come to me for guidance on connecting with Faerie and returned to share the results of following my advice.

· · · · · · ·

This book is about fact, not lore, although some people may have difficulty accepting that.

I was raised in the tradition (custom) of my mother, who learned from her mother. For me it was mostly learning by example and copying what my mother did, then later augmenting, expanding upon, or tailoring things to my personal energy and interests. In some ways this book provides that type of guidance for the reader. Take what you are drawn to, experiment with care, but remember that your Craft is individualized by your energy, so you should follow your intuition as to how to personalize your magical work. I have written about my practice in my books on Green Witchcraft, magic, tarot, and more, but I have not gone into a great deal of information about the Fairie connection of the Old Religion until now.

I grew up with spirits coming and going at home, and as a child I would set out milk for the fairies on the full moon, make grass houses for the fairies, acknowledge the power of the local flowers and herbs, and talk to plants and animals, and I thought that everyone lived the same way. I was raised to understand omens, dreams, visions, moving energy, and working with the Other People without it being a formal training; it was simply a matter of course and following the example of my mother. When I was in second grade, a group of us little girls talked about what we did over the weekend, and when it was my turn, I said we set out milk for the fairies under the full moon. One girl replied with contempt, "That's what witches do!" That afternoon I told my mother about this and asked, "Mommy, are we witches?" She answered in a low voice with measured tones that I recognized as her way of telling me that what she was saying was *important*: "We never name ourselves. Others name us. And those who need us will find us." Certain moments in my life are inscribed in my memory with absolute clarity, and this is one of those. Highly detailed memories and dreams are sublime moments of great personal significance, bringing the subconscious into contact with the conscious, and are worthy of being treasured while also offering an insight into Faerie communication.

As I grew older, my mother's words took on further meaning. In her day and that of her mother, the Old Religion was maintained in silence beneath the surface of the new because persecution, whether violent or merely community shunning, was always a threat. Even so, people knew who to go to for help and healing when the normal avenues failed to bring the desired results. Money was not exchanged for these services, but reciprocation was understood and came in the form of useful gifts, food, or manual labor. The names that others give us can become a definition, something that encapsulates their expectations of us in a shell of their own design. Names become a tool to mentally organize the environment, interactions, and relationships, but they can also put limits on understanding and hamper experience.

I was also raised with a pantheistic and animistic worldview. Everything has Divine Spirit in it, so everything is alive, and thus we can communicate with anything. As an adult I once sat on a large boulder on an isolated hill overlooking a panoramic vista. I patted the rock and said, "You have a terrific view here." In my mind I heard a definite, concise response: "Used to be better." Being quite alone there, I looked around and noticed that behind me and the boulder there was grassy indentation in the ground showing that in the distant past the boulder had slid a few yards down the hillside. Indeed, the view had once been better. I gave "him" another pat and poured the boulder a libation from my bottle of spring water before I continued on my way. Everything has energy—atoms in motion—and we trade off electrons with the objects and beings around us. In the case of the boulder, I felt its serene, heavy energy and its being in the moment, without plans or concerns, taking our short interaction as a matter of course.

Witches generally shield themselves with the energy of a visualized surrounding light so as not to pick up unwanted energies, or they smudge themselves with the smoke of burning sage, rosemary, or lavender after a negative encounter to clear their energy field. Many energy-sensitive people also carry crystals or stones whose energies they identify as precautionary protection, letting the stone's natural energies enhance personal shielding, or ward off negativity. As long as you are not acting out of fearfulness, a little shielding is fine, but don't cut yourself off from all contact or you might miss out on special moments that aid in your spiritual growth.

When people talk about creating your own reality, witches understand that you must *know* it, not believe it, for this to be successful. Throughout my childhood and until I went to college, my mother recited to me her own mother's rules for conducting magic, which I call the Rules of Conduct. These are the words she spoke to me in that significant tone and modulation (capitalization shows her emphasis):

Be careful what you do.

Be careful who you trust.

4

Do not use the Power to hurt another,
for what is SENT comes back.

Never use the Power against someone who HAS the
Power, for you both draw from the same well.

To use the Power, you must FEEL it in your
heart and KNOW it in your mind.

This book is a compilation of things I have not written about—or an expansion on what I have written about—and is intended for those who need it or are open to it. It is about the Other People and Otherworld, also called Faerie. One of the features of the Old Religion, particularly from my perspective, is the acknowledgment of the Other People, no matter by what name they are called. Familiar terms for the Other People may be derived from the Old English word for "strange" or a shortened form of Fair Folk, fairy, fairy folk, faerie folk, or fae, and are generally used interchangeably to describe the Other People, but fairy is mostly used to designate a being. The word *fey* means "doomed to die soon" or "ill-omened" but has come into use to be associated with fairy, as with the charming *Fey Tarot Deck*, or a malevolent fairy being, as may be found in certain role-playing games (such as Forgotten Realms). Use of fey may stem from a tradition that sees the Fair Folk as dangerous and ominous toward people who are not in attunement with them.

The term *Faerie* was introduced in the sixteenth century by Spenser in his epic *The Faerie Queene*, during the reign of Queen Elizabeth I of England, meaning the Otherworld, although it has also come to mean the individual inhabitants. The Faerie of Spenser was an imaginary place occupied by imaginary inhabitants. The usual view of scholars presents the Other People of the Old Religion as the old gods, whose importance diminished with the advent of the New Religion. At one point the Pagan gods were redefined and integrated into the new hierarchy as fallen angels who failed to choose a side in the war between God and

Lucifer ("light-bringer" in ancient Roman, meaning Venus as the morning star). They were too good for Hell (a curiously fiery location named for Hel, the Norse goddess of the icy underworld) but not good enough for Heaven (located somewhere "out there" in space beyond the planet) and eventually became identified as demons, then were further reduced in size with the Victorian Age advent of cute, tiny human-looking beings with butterfly wings, and finally determined to be nonexistent save as creatures of whimsy or as an ancient people like the Picts or as the fancy of the mentally unstable. Curiously, demons (from the Greek word *daimon*, meaning "spirit") and devils were attested to be real and certainly to be avoided or exorcised by the appropriate church authorities.

The Sidhe (usually pronounced *shee*, meaning "mound" or "hill") are the fairy folk said to dwell in great feasting halls under the ancient mounds of Ireland. Often associated with spirits, the word is also seen in *banshee* (sidhe woman), the ghostly figure of a wailing woman (sometimes washing bloody linen) who foretells a death. The nobility of the Sidhe are called the Daoine Sidhe (pronounced like *dee'na shee*), and the whole group has been linked to a people called the Tuatha de Danann (*Too'ah day Dan'ann*), the people of (the goddess) Danu, who took Ireland from the Fir Bolgs only to lose it centuries later to the Milesians—the Gaelic Celts—about 1000 BCE ("before the Common Era" is used by many historians instead of BC, "before Christ," in deference to worldwide cultural and spiritual differences). The word *Sidhe* is becoming more popular in describing the Other People, particularly the elves.

According to legend, the Sidhe put up such a good fight that the invading Celts were impressed and came to a truce, giving the Sidhe kings the right to live under the hills (*sidhes*) that are abundant in Ireland, although some of them chose instead to dwell under the sea or in lands west of the sea. Today the fairy hills are believed to be burial mounds, but excavations are discouraged, just in case they are not. The Irish have a special feeling for the Little People, the Good Neighbors, and do not like anyone, especially outsiders, disturbing the hills lest the Fair Ones become angered and dangerous.

Are fairies a different species living in a parallel world, connected to this world at the earth's natural ley lines of magnetic pulses, and able to travel between dimensions? Are they a people so mysterious that the only description that suits them is to say that they are *Other*? Are they the elementals in a visible form? Are they the remnants of ancient tribes such as the Picts? Are they fallen angels or the spirits of the dead or the spirits of the land, plants, and animals? Or are they the diminished form of ancient deities? All of these ideas have been considered by Neopagans, theologians, poets, archaeologists, and historians, but the fact that historical people (such as William the Conqueror) are said to have married someone of this race suggests that there will continue to be many interpretations for the Sidhe.

Accepting the strange as normal is a challenge to our worldview.

In Celtic lands, a hovering or moving light seen in a marshy place is still called a fairy fire or elf light and is said to be the soul of a dead warrior or a child (a corpse candle), illustrating the association of fairies with the spirits of the dead. These lights can be explained away as caused by atmospheric conditions and the igniting of gases, such as methane,

emanating from decaying plant or animal matter, yet they have been associated with fairies for centuries, and not all sightings are so easily dismissed. Accepting the strange as normal is a challenge to our worldview, so instead we humans tend to categorize and explain things to fit known patterns. Nevertheless, up to the present there are still a sufficient number of experiences of daylight fairy encounters to imply a different race or at least a people with abilities not common to most modern humans.

To be honest, I cringe a bit every time in this book where I use the words Faerie, fairy, fairy folk, or fair ones—which is a reaction the Other People find quite gratifying. These words are what humans commonly use to describe a people who may appear bright, pale, shining, glowing, gossamer, and so on, otherwise called individually elves, sprites, nature spirits, and a myriad of other names for entities that are not human yet are familiar to cultures worldwide. When teaching classes on my family tradition of Witchcraft, I include a class on fairies, so I asked the Other People if it would be okay for me to use the word *fairy* since people are familiar with this term. (The fair folk speak whatever language the human speaks in making contact, so you don't have to learn Gaelic or any other language, foreign or antiquated, such as Latin, to communicate with them; it's the same thing with deities.) There was a resigned response of "We're used to it, but we really don't like it."

They consider the various fairy terms patronizing, as though they were children being patted on the head by a doting adult, which is completely opposite of reality. They tend to laugh knowingly when I use the offensive words in my classes, aware that my language paradigm has been significantly altered. This little lesson also emphasizes the truth that when working with the Other People, words have *meanings*, and you will need to keep that in mind.

· · · · · · · ·

This book may possibly open the way for personal contact with a very real people in a very real Otherworld.

This is the kind of book you are reading—one that may alter your worldview and possibly open the way for personal contact with a very real people in a very real Otherworld. This book is not about fiction, cosplay, gaming, fantasy, dress-up, or role-playing; it covers real events, real encounters, how to encourage contact, how to navigate the nuances of communication, how to back out graciously if needed, and how to apologize when appropriate. I have not written about this before simply because it is also dangerous for the inept, which I have been on occasion, so I can speak from experience. This book is appropriate for the advanced practitioner of any esoteric Craft, be it Witchcraft, Wicca, Heathenism, Asatru, Shamanism, or general Paganism. This is not a dissertation on the fairy faith, nor is it a compilation of fairy lore, explaining the various types of Faerie denizens, as these subjects have already been well addressed by W. Y. Evans-Wentz's

The Fairy Faith in Celtic Countries and by Katharine Briggs in her excellent *An Encyclopedia of Fairies*. Instead, this is a book of secrets, describing personal experiences, encounters, mind-set and heart-set, how to open the way for those who would like to work with the Other People, and how to work magic.

I will use terms like *Spirit* and *Universe*, which are subject to individual interpretation, allowing you to conceptualize them as the Divine, the Goddess and the God, the Supreme Being, Ultimate Source, and so on, and thus can be applied to any spiritual or religious worldview. The Universe is not about outer space, filled with galaxies and going about doing whatever it is that universes do, but is here regarded as the undefinable Universe, the Infinite Light, the Divine. This view is conceptualized in the charming story about the god Shiva and goddess Parvati and the sibling rivalry of their two sons: Skanda, the younger, slim, multi-armed God of War, and Ganesh, the older, plump, elephant-headed Remover of Obstacles. Skanda challenged Ganesh to a race around the world, with whomever returning first to their parents' side becoming recognized as their number one son. Ganesh, with approval from Shiva and Parvati, agreed. Skanda took off like a shot and vanished into the distance, but Ganesh simply stood up and walked around his parents, saying, "You are all the world to me." They were charmed and declared him the winner, so that when Skanda returned, out of breath, he was shocked to see he had lost the race and Ganesh was still the number one son. For me, the Goddess and the God, separate or together, are the Universe— the all-encompassing Divine Spirit, intelligent, loving, infinite. When you consider the word *infinite*, remember that we do not live in a closed universe, but one in which energy is always available. Although we may not understand the dynamics of the universe, we know that black holes consume and expel matter and energy, that there is energy and dark energy, that there is matter and dark matter, and that there is a great deal we have yet to learn.

While what I write about is based on my own perspective and my experiences, as well as those of people who have confided these to me, you may have completely different but equally valid experiences, for we each make our own unique contacts. There will be some statements in quotations, without reference. That is just how it is in Witchcraft; sources and people are not always identified, especially in a book that is open to the public. There may be times when I put a word in quotations or italics without explanation, and perhaps you will grasp the meaning at once or you will need to read further to learn more about it. The events in this book do not describe theory or belief, but actual occurrences, for in the Craft belief is not necessary because one *knows*. I recommend tabbing those parts of the book that you will want to refer back to, such as types of circle casting, rituals, crafts, and meditations. If you are uncertain about opening the door to a different reality, stop reading now. Otherwise, proceed with caution.

. . . .

If you are uncertain about opening the door to a different reality, stop reading now.

I feel it is *critically important* to note here that no drugs of any kind, and no alcohol, need be ingested or otherwise taken to make contact and communicate with the Divine, the Other People, spirits, ascended masters, guardian spirits, or guardian angels, so that you are alert and fully aware of your connection and there is nothing artificial that can be ascribed to your very real experiences. If you prefer drugs or alcohol, that is a personal choice.

chapter 1

The Reality of Faerie

The actual existence of a Fairy Realm or Otherworld is sometimes lost in a fog of wistfulness, with literary and cinematic constructs defining the territory in a myriad of patterns. There are so many images to draw upon, so many illustrations and concepts, that it is easy to believe Faerie must appear like any one of these and the inhabitants must behave as has been projected into our consciousness by artists, writers, and cinematographers. Yet what we see and read comes from a single person's visualization of a storyline that can be as fantastical or strange as the person can create. But what if you don't have to create Faerie? Suppose it simply IS.

Faerie Is Real

"Oh my god, the matrix changed!" the middle-aged student shouted to the rest of the class. This was the reaction of a skeptic experiencing a paradigm shift in one of my Faerie classes. To be clear right from the start, this heading is not a metaphor; it is a statement. I have found that it

doesn't matter how much or in what manner I prepare my students for the reality of Otherworld and the Other People, nor does it matter if students are skeptics or enthusiasts; some will accept and even embrace the shift, and others will barricade themselves against it with shielding, denial, or analytical deconstruction and reconstruction of their experience until it becomes more intellectually manageable. The opening exclamation from one of my students is a case in point for the latter. If you desire to have an Otherworld encounter, you must be willing to accept that it is possible to achieve—not with gritted teeth and girded loins, but with a calm demeanor and a loving heart, for Love really is the Law, and Love really is the Bond.

The episode from the above paragraph began with one of the classes in my Green Witchcraft thirteen-lesson course. The focus for this installment was Faerie, and there were twenty-five enthusiastic students ranging in age from mid-twenties to mid-sixties. After talking about communicating with the Other People, I took a portal stone from a small pouch I carry with me, looked at my friend within, and asked if it was okay for me to let the students see him. I was given permission, so I took the stone around the circle of students for each to look into. What they saw was a person facing them, mounted on a horse that looked like a cross between the Andalusian and Mongolian breeds, standing on a trail in a small clearing within a woodland.

The first person in the circle commented with satisfaction, "Oh yes, I can see how the matrix inside the stone makes it look like there's a man on a horse." I made no reply and continued around the circle, showing the stone to all the students. When I finished, I quietly asked my friend in the stone if he would change the scene and allow me to take the stone around again. He smiled, gently turned his steed around, and started back toward the forest. I took the stone, without saying what was depicted in it, and began to make the rounds again, and that was when the first student was shocked and blurted out the statement about the matrix having changed. Everyone in the class saw the original scene, and they all saw the second scene too. Some students were clearly excited, while others seemed unsettled by the change.

I put away that stone and brought out another portal stone to see who was there, for this stone was not dedicated to my friend. The scene was a small group of males sitting behind a campfire in a forest opening and enjoying a beverage. One held up his wood tankard in greeting. In the foreground was a tall slender shining white lady with her back to me. I quietly greeted the people within and asked permission to show the stone to my students, and the lady turned to look at me and nodded her consent.

I took this stone around the circle, but some of the students were approaching overload. Two of them who had originally been excited about connecting with Faerie recoiled before the stone and became so overheated that they began to sweat profusely. They had water bottles and cooled off quickly as I moved on. Putting that stone away, I continued with the class. I have found that there is usually at least one student in a class who is initially eager to make contact with fairies, only to discover that having Faerie taken from a fun fantasy into a reality is unexpected and shocking.

Having Faerie taken from a fun fantasy into a reality is unexpected and shocking.

I have seen similar energy reactions in my class on making and using a black mirror, or when I use one in a dark moon or sidhe moon esbat. Some people react with overheating when discovering that black mirror portals actually work, and it seems to me that the heat may come from friction between the person's auric field and the Otherworld gateway. Perhaps the person unconsciously puts up an energy shield or there is an automatic reaction from the physical body to something strange and possibly threatening. This may simply indicate that the individual is not ready for an Otherworld encounter or resists having a preconceived notion overturned by an actual event. In such cases, the person simply steps back from the portal and the body temperature immediately returns to normal.

The terms Faerie, Fairie, Fairyland, fairy, and fae are the words people are familiar with and use most when speaking of the Otherworld and the inhabitants, and so I may use them occasionally in this book up to a point. By now most of the Other People I have encountered are kinda-sorta okay with these terms, and while they understand our limitations, they are not enthusiastic about the appellations, as mentioned in the introduction. I will use mostly the words Sidhe or Other People when writing about them throughout the book.

If you desire to interact with the Other People, you must do so with the right mind-set and heart-set.

The Other People generally prefer such names as Good Neighbors, Shining Ones, Other, and even Friend or Companion. If you desire to interact with the Other People, you must do so with the right mind-set and heart-set. Perfect Love and Perfect Trust define the heart and mind coordinated and uninhibited by prejudices or expectations. Considering that the interpretation of Faerie has been overwritten in the past couple of thousand years by people who were highly biased against the Other People, those cultural perspectives need to be put aside in order to have a relationship with them. It is difficult to form a bond with a people you intend to manipulate for your own ends or who you think could really be demonic beings (in the sense of evil). The Otherworld should only be entered with a loving heart-set and trusting mind-set, for this is one of the major rules of connecting with Faerie: what you take into Otherworld is what you will find there.

How Portals Work

I mentioned portal stones and black mirror portals, so what are these? Portals are gateways or entrances to another world. In Irish tradition the portal may be a hill or a fairy mound (sidhe), although Neolithic standing stones, stone circles, or dolmen formations (two portal stones, a capstone, and usually a back stone so the top sits on three pillars) may also be gateways. In other locations the portal could be a hidden cleft in a mountain side (as with the tale of the Pied Piper of Hamlin), a sacred pool or spring, and caves. However, a portal can be anywhere, and they can come and go.

Portal stones are gemstones that show a different world or individuals when you look into it. Not everyone will see a world or people, so if you do, it is because you were meant to—rather like receiving an invitation that you may accept or decline as you choose. Remember that the choice is always yours. For gemstone portals to Otherworld, I have three polished semiprecious fluorites, 1½ inches in size, with smooth centers and faceted edges. I keep them in individual velveteen pouches and always keep one close by. Other stones that I have used as portals are pietersite, quartz crystal, picture jasper, and labradorite.

For me, labradorite tends to be a gateway to the Underworld, the realm of the Lord and Lady of Shadows. I use this stone for connecting with those who have passed over or for gaining information from the god and goddess of that realm. My pietersite is a high-energy stone in which I usually see views of beautiful mountainous landscapes, sometimes with people traversing at a distance or with people nearby and willing to interact. Quartz crystal has a range of uses, so beings can appear in them and messages can be transmitted. I was once drawn to a softball-size quartz point for sale in my shop while a customer was browsing various other stones. I looked inside it and saw a bright winged being who self-identified as Archangel Gabriel and told me to tell the customer a single word. I am used to spirits insisting that I say something to someone, so I shrugged and said, "I just received a message for you from Archangel

Gabriel, and I've been told to say to you _____." The person burst into tears and hugged me tightly, saying, "That is EXACTLY what I needed to hear!"

The person then told me about frequently praying to Archangel Gabriel for consolation and advice, and that the one word answered the most recent prayer, allowing for moving on in life. It seems to me that the image and message were designed solely for the benefit of the intended recipient. The word *angel* translates as "messenger," and angelic winged beings have been part of the Old Religion worldwide going as far back as the religions of ancient India, Sumer and Babylon, Greece and Rome, and even the Birdmen Sect of Easter Island, to name only a few examples. I am not placing a definition on the being who gave me the message to deliver; however, I am confident the message was genuine and needed to be delivered at that time.

A portal is also a means of looking into another dimension where you can contact a spirit guide, ascended master, ancestors, deities, or see your own past lives. Do you need a portal to see into the Otherworld? Not necessarily, but it is convenient. A portal within an object seems to present a glimpse of a dimensional shift within a confined space. There are many roads and many destinations, so different gemstones might access different spaces at different times. One of my fluorites used to show a woodland view but after a couple of years altered to show a desert region and an elephantine creature, and later on the scene changed yet again. This is important, for it indicates that this particular portal moves around in Otherworld.

A scene within a portal may also appear to be frozen in time until deliberately accessed. By looking into an active/activated portal stone for a time, the scene is set into motion rather like watching a slow-motion old-fashioned silent movie. Sounds, if any, come to the mind rather than the ear. Scenes shift slowly, demonstrating that time passes differently in that world compared to this one. Part of the uncanny sensation that people experience with Otherworld contact may come from this temporal shift as the two temporal zones brush up against each other. Time flies or crawls depending on one's perspective. With some stones, the view may be similar to looking through a thin veil. Fluorites have patterns and may have stripes of color in greens, blues, yellows, and purples of varying intensity from pale to deep toned, so the images may appear to be taking place behind the stone's overlaying pattern.

The idea of temporal shifts in Otherworld can be found in folktales. The story of Rip Van Winkle shows a journey into Faerie for a night of drinking and playing nine pins (an early form of bowling), but when he woke the next morning, decades had passed. Herla's Rade, an English tale, speaks of a lord and his entourage attending a Fairy wedding, and on departing the next day was told by his host to carry a little dog with him and dismount only when the dog jumped off. When one of his men became annoyed with the delay and dismounted, he turned to dust, so the rest of the men rode the skies, waiting for the dog to leap off, and continue to ride for fear of the same fate. It would appear that the one person dismounting threw the process out of sequence, resulting in a temporal trap. So, when you are told to do something a certain way by the Other People, it would probably be the wisest course, but it is always a personal choice.

The Rade is also called the Wild Hunt, led by different people depending on the culture (rade is Scottish for "road"). It could be led by the Welsh God of the Underworld, Gwyn ap Nudd, gathering the spirits of the dead in stormy weather to carry them to their rest until rebirth. The leader is usually referred to as the Hunter and could be Odin/Woden, Hecate, Hulda, the Valkyrie (led by Freya), Herne the Hunter, King Arthur, historical figures (Charlemagne), biblical figures (Enoch), and so on. People seeing or coming into contact with the Wild Hunt could be swept up in the Rade and carried off to Faerie or the Underworld. The Hunter is seen as the one who gathers the spirits of the dead and takes them to the Underworld, thus he may well be an aspect of the Lord of Shadows, the God of the Underworld. While a person can ask to ride with the Rade, there is no guarantee of a safe return unless the ride is taken in Perfect Love and Perfect Trust.[1]

Dimensional Shifts in Everyday Life

Portals may simply occur unexpectedly in otherwise ordinary circumstances. I have had this experience more than once and I have learned that this has happened with others as well. I have driven down a familiar road, for example, in the early evening, when I feel an odd sensation and realize that I no longer recognize my surroundings. I keep driving and eventually the sensation fades and the scenery is once more familiar. I have not felt any sense of alarm but instead find it intriguing while simply continuing on my way. When discussing the phenomenon with others, some respond with descriptions of similar experiences, from a familiar road becoming unfamiliar to passing through a town at night where all the windows were lit up only to discover on the return daylight trip that no town is there. It appears that portals from other dimensions also move around in this world, just as happens with my fluorite portal stone to Otherworld.

Curiously, common to all the experiences related to me, as well as my own, is the lack of people or other vehicles and the sensation that the area was desolate, strange, and uninviting. I don't know what would happen if a person stopped in these kinds of situations to investigate their surroundings, but perhaps a person might end up in a different time, dimension, or universe. Another aspect of this is finding that what should be a short trip feels much longer while experiencing that unfamiliar sensation. One person told me about seeing a man apparently wearing a black suit in a wooded area walking toward the road, but the closer the man came, the shorter he got, until at last, as the person drove past, a black cat was sitting at the side of the road, watching.

---

1   To help people understand the nature of this journey, I wrote a meditation for riding with the Rade in *Green Witchcraft II*.

It seems reasonable that a person's body chemistry will react to things not being quite right when brushing up against a portal accidentally, thus triggering the uncanny, eerie sensation that warns a person to keep moving. The strange sensation could be caused by the energies not being aligned between "that" world and "this" body. As with people who get overheated in front of a black mirror or gemstone portal, there is friction when a person is up against the veil between the worlds and is unwilling to engage in further contact. It may be the physical body's way of sending a signal that this is no longer an ordinary or physically familiar territory, so being in tune with your body, trusting the sense it emits that something doesn't feel normal, and paying attention to this may be a cautionary communication from Spirit or the Divine, by whatever name or identification a person embraces. The fact that the road becomes not only unfamiliar but emits an unusual energy indicates this place is currently not for you.

There are other worlds and dimensions that may be accessed if and when necessary.

For me such incidents usually occur around twilight, during the grayness just before either sunset or sunrise, which is traditionally associated with fairy encounters as well as with interaction between our world and Otherworld. This type of incident may also occur in the dark of night, usually around midnight, an hour associated with Otherworld as well as with magical workings and spirit communication. When stumbling into an intersection of worlds or dimensions, action may not be required; simply continuing on your way may be the best response. Trust your intuition and consider this an opportunity to know that portals exist, thus demonstrating that there are other worlds and dimensions that may be accessed if and when necessary. People tend to have more than one such experience and while initially they might find it unsettling, they usually become calmer about it with subsequent encounters. It seems that multiple exposure to portals helps people become acclimated to the unusual, and possibly these portals will open into vistas more inviting to the participant and offer people a safe haven in another dimension at a time of dire need.

What Is Otherworld?

Use the word Otherworld in the same way you would use the word Earth. We talk about the earth and about Earth, so sometimes the article "the" is appropriate and other times it is not necessary. Otherworld is also referred to as Faerie or Fairyland and is a world where the Other People normally dwell. It is a place that can be accessed by request, meditation, portals of various types, astral projection, and what are termed lucid dreams (*lucid* in the actual meaning of clarity and being readily understood). It also is a land that can overlay this world. It seems that Otherworld is accessible to this world through venues that work differently for each individual. Locations exist around the world that are recognized as gateways, even if not currently functional, and may be places where the Otherworld is in closer alignment to this world. The Puerta de Hayu Marca in Peru is an ancient doorway carved as a mere recess into a solid rock wall, but it is still believed by the local people to be a portal to another dimension, the place through which the deities came and went long ago.

There are places around the world where local legends and customs indicate a sacred place where people can be contacted by the Divine or where the Other People can enter and leave this world. Perhaps these are places where in the past people frequently passed back and forth through portals between these two worlds, as is suggested by legends in various cultures. It is also possible that the strange and often unsettling sensations people feel when a portal simply opens up are caused by shifts in the electromagnetic field. Since the planet is currently experiencing a shift of the magnetic poles, the earth may become unsettled, with dynamic changes occurring to the land, and thus the portals are becoming more active in preparation for safe exits.

People who disappear from plain sight, for example, may or may not return, depending on their mind-set and heart-set and on the situation at hand. I know of a case where a child around the age of eight was playing outdoors with a toy unicorn when the watchful parent realized the child had simply vanished. No sense of alarm came to the parent, who simply "knew" that the child was safe and would soon return. A few moments later the child reappeared. Later the parent recounted the experience to the child, and the child claimed to have gone to play with the white unicorns and that it was the parent who had disappeared. After romping with the unicorns for a time, the child decided it was time to return home, at which point the unicorns disappeared and the parent reappeared—two different perspectives of the same event involving a dimensional crossover. Note also that the child played awhile, then decided it was time to go home, but barely any time had passed from the parent's perspective. When children are raised in an open-minded environment, there is less chance for fear to enter their thoughts. Instead, what prevails is the ability to sense the energies and have a relaxed acceptance that all is well. That is an example of mind-set, and it is also Perfect Trust. The concept of positive thoughts attracting positive results is well-founded. Negative thoughts generate fears that take root in the mind, and although not in the physical realm, such a mind-set can draw that energy to a person. There are many self-help and psychology books about the relationship between how we think and how we live.

Beings from the Otherworld are also able to enter this world and interact with people, but usually there is an accompanying sensation of something being slightly odd about them. I've experienced three encounters by three different elderly men who out of the blue approached me and gave me the same message. With this type of encounter, there is a definite sense of the meaningfulness of words. This took place in three different locations, in three different states, over a period of three years. With each occasion I felt the power and energy of these beings, and I absolutely knew they were messengers from Otherworld.

People tend to brush aside the existence of numinous things until defined by some scientist or physicist, and then the definition becomes the parameter of the experience or thing. I prefer to go with my intuition, and when working with the Other People, I feel this is probably the best way. Psychology tells us that we are always living in the past because the brain is not actually aware of things until the message is received from the body's transmitters. When someone speaks to you, it takes a fraction of a second for that to travel from ear to brain. When you touch something hot, your body short-circuits the brain by going directly into the spinal cord nerves so you jerk your hand away, then your brain realizes what happened. I actually find this amusing only because so many people talk about "living in the now"—but actually, we never do. There is past and future in our mental cognizance, but not present; it is always a memory of what was present, hence is now past. To live in the present, the now, may require trusting intuition *before* it registers in the mind.

There are aspects of the Otherworld that merge into this world and become defined as the paranormal, psychic awareness, second sight, the supernatural, and so on. It is important to understand that there may indeed be an interconnection, so there is no point in confining parts of your life into definition capsules, for all your experiences are part of you. I tend not to define who is or is not a resident of the Otherworld, or whether a being is an elf, a sprite, or a spirit entity, although they may identify themselves as such or seem to fit a familiar description. There are meditative familiar paths into that land, for example, but I feel it is more rewarding to be surprised and enlightened by encounters than to have a set idea of who should or should not be there.

What does this world look like from the Otherworld? On a full moon long ago, I started drumming while sitting alone on the back porch, looking at the moon. A tune with unknown words came to me, which I sang to the moon, to the Goddess, as I drummed. I don't know what I sang or what the tune was once I had finished, but I remember that it was beautiful, that I was delighted that my voice carried the tune perfectly, and I knew at the time that the song was my offering to the Goddess. I heard her ask what I would like in return, and I said, "I would like to know how this world looks from Otherworld." In an instant the scenery changed. The best way to describe it is that the trees, the large and small shrubs, and everything in the large backyard became like cardboard cutouts— one-dimensional, flat, and upright, staggered across a flat surface, rather like a greeting card that when opened pops up to show what passes for a three-dimensional scene. Beyond this I saw the Otherworld as a genuine three-dimensional landscape of brilliant, rich colors and vast expanse, gorgeous beyond description. The image disappeared and my yard returned to normal. Decades later, a group of physicists announced that the universe is a hologram and everything is actually flat, but we don't perceive this because we are in it (run *holographic universe* in an internet search engine for some fun reading). When visiting Otherworld, watch out for wandering physicists.

When you visit Otherworld, watch out for wandering physicists.

Because the Otherworld and this world can overlap, it is difficult to say where exactly it is located. I would surmise it to be in a parallel dimension with staggered openings, crossovers, or over-lays to this dimension and possibly other ones. There appear to be links between this world and the Otherworld dimension at certain junctures around the world, places that have a reputation for strange energies or ghostly apparitions such as figures on horseback or on foot who move into view and disappear. These junctures may be bridges between the dimensions, or shortcuts from one spot in Otherworld to another, such as with legendary fairy roads. We may see or feel this dimensional presence from time to time, and I recommend taking a calm approach, such as when the familiar becomes unfamiliar, just keep going about your business.

I also recommend not staring at someone you feel is Other as traditionally they are not open to this. Perhaps staring comes across as being intrusive or even aggressive. Additionally, they might be annoyed at being discovered, and there are tales of people getting eye damage or blindness from staring at the Other People in this world. Perhaps there is a radiation reaction, similar to staring at the sun or a laser light. You can glance at the sun, but if you stare, you will burn a hole in your retina, leaving a blind spot in your vision. What I call mind-set and heart-set helps you to achieve a calm, non-intrusive response to an interaction with Otherworld.

Mind-set is an open mind, neither judgmental nor overly inquisitive, but reacting with the mental consideration that *this is normal.* Savor the moment(s) and soon you will be able to move peacefully with the energy flow. Heart-set is about being compassionate and empathic, reacting with sincere consideration for the feelings and possible fears of others, with the sensation of *warmth and love.* It is all about understanding the words "Perfect Love and Perfect Trust." This expression is familiar to most Pagans, as are the words "Love is the Law and Love is the Bond." These phrases regularly show up in Pagan rituals, and I use them as well.

The more one practices the Craft, the more likely it is that deities will simply turn up when you need advice or assistance, so keep an open mind and don't feel you have to limit yourself to one pantheon. Once when I was pondering a magical decision, Cerridwen appeared and I instantly understood what would be the consequences of whichever choice I made: immediate but short-lived results or delayed but long-term results. When I picked immediate, she gently asked me, "Are you sure?" and I said I was, and things went as indicated. Key here is the knowledge that what we do is of our own free will; it is our choice, and I can live with that. Part of witchcraft is taking responsibility for your actions, being grateful for assistance, and making amends when needed.

Elementals As Otherworld Powers

Most Pagans are familiar with the cardinal directions (north, east, south, and west) and with the elementals that rule these regions (Earth, Air,

Fire, and Water). I consider the elementals to be powers that we can communicate with and encounter. I have heard some Pagans compare the elementals to three-year-old children who need to be told what to do and kept under control, but I feel this does not take into account their power as earthquakes, tornadoes, volcanic eruptions, and hurricanes. In one Craft book, I came across a chant to banish unexpected spirit visitors. After reading this I went to bed that night and awoke to see four shadowy, robed, and hooded figures standing at the foot of my bed. The banishing chant came to mind, but then I thought, "But that's rude." So instead I raised my hands, palms outward, to them and said, "I give you my blessing, but I am very tired and cannot stay awake." The four shadowy figures immediately changed position, with one standing at my head, one at my feet, and the other two at either side. They raised their arms and extended very long shadowy fingers to form a square over me, touching their own thumbs and each other's little fingers. I thought, "Oh! Foursquare! You're the elementals!" They lowered their hands in unison over me and raised them again, then vanished, leaving me to feel happy, blessed, and able to go right back to sleep. This is an example of heart-set, for I could not be rude to even unknown shadowy spirits who had obviously made a point of coming to see me. Perhaps this was a test to see my reaction, and apparently they approved of my response to their impromptu visit and of my letting them know that my physical form was tired.

Take responsibility for your actions, be grateful for assistance, and make amends when needed.

A few days after my bedtime encounter with the elementals, I was in a store looking for a specific style and design in a thin scarf that I could use as a table cover. Attached to a wall in the store was a wooden rod fully packed with a large number of scarves knotted on it and hanging down. I could not see any that resembled what I had envisioned, so as a test (and therein lies balance), I called upon the elementals to help me find the scarf, and simply stuck my hand into the mass of scarves, grabbed something out of sight, and pulled it forward, only to discover it was exactly what I sought. This was so delightful that I played with the elementals and kept asking for more scarves, with each one I described coming to my hand in the same unseen way. I laughed at our successful game and said I had better stop now since I had to pay for these. The point is that the elementals are part of us and we are part of them, so give respect and friendship if that is what you desire to receive in return.

I view the elementals as our kith and kin, very close relatives. We have body and strength, we are kith and kin to Earth; we have breath and thought, we are kith and kin to Air; we have heat and vitality, we are kith and kin to Fire; and we have fluids and emotions, we are kith and kin to Water. When I call upon the elementals in ritual, I use the same format with each of them, inserting the above kinship associations:

> *I call upon you, elemental _____, to attend*
> *this rite and guard this circle, for as I (or "we"*
> *for a group) have _____, I am (we are)*
> *your kith and kin. Hail and welcome!*

When bidding them farewell, I simply say:

> *Depart in peace, elemental _____ (Earth,*
> *Air, Fire, Water). My (our) blessings*
> *take with you. Hail and farewell!*

In terms of quarters, I am convinced that there are indeed rulers for each quadrant of the Otherworld, who are perhaps powerful Otherworldly kings and queens, rulers like dukes and duchesses under an overall king and queen, or who are the God and the Goddess in their aspects of Queen and King of Otherworld, since the Divine is present in all dimensions and universes. The regions of Otherworld can even be related to the seasons, with a ruling king and queen for each season. You are free to choose names for them from one or more mythologies that appeal to you, with a couple of examples being Titania and Oberon or

Mab and Fearn. I tend to such terms as Lord and Lady of Nature, Lord of the Wildwood and Lady of the Fields, God and Goddess of the Green-wood, and King and Queen of Otherworld.

For regular rituals, I set my altar and start my circle casting at the north because I see this as the realm of the Crone Goddess, and thus of wisdom. For Otherworld rituals, I set up the altar at the west, as this is associated with learning and knowledge, but also with eternity and regeneration, and thus with Otherworld in the Celtic Ogham system of fews, which are used like runes for writing and divination.[2] The west was also seen as the land of the spirits in ancient Egypt, with tombs in the Valley of the Kings on the west side of the Nile, so contact with spirits as well as the Other People can occur here, and the circle casting for an Otherworld ritual differs from the usual.

Temporal and Dimensional Shifts

It is important to understand that time is different from what we are usually taught. It is not lineal but more like a spiral that you can dip into at certain points. When in the Otherworld, I have felt that events take place as they normally should: walking a distance takes the usual amount of time expected, for example, but when returning to this world, I see that only a few minutes have passed. This is especially true with medita-tive travels and black mirror travels.

Time will move depending on your perspective, and it will not be consistent. If anything, Otherworld presents contradictions, for while events there may move at a slow pace and here it moves more quickly, the reverse can also be true. As with the unicorn adventure of the child and parent, the time in this world may seem to move slower than that of Otherworld, but when gazing in a portal, the reverse may appear to be true to the viewer as the visions move slowly and gracefully, whereas to the inhabitants, their time must seem normal and perhaps ours is slow. There is a theory of Otherworld being a reverse image of this world, with

2 See *Green Witchcraft II* and *Grimoire for the Green Witch*.

the seasons in reverse as well; however, it is also possible that seasons are influenced by location, such as the quarter realms relating to the elementals: north/winter, east/spring, south/summer, and west/autumn.

The phenomenon of time noticeably slowing down has been associated with accidents and other seriously dangerous events from which people survive and wonder how they did that. A friend told me about being in a car wreck but during that moment, time slowed down and a glowing light enveloped the car. The absolute knowledge that all would be well came to mind, and there was time for my friend to shift position in the car to avoid the worst of the accident. I once was driving on a busy two-lane highway when a car pulled out from a side street and stopped in front of me while the driver looked for an opening in the opposite lane. I saw the car behind it coming up to the stop sign, saw the gap between the two cars, and was able to "dance" my car behind the one that blocked my lane and in front of the one coming to the sign. I flashed a smile at the driver approaching the stop sign on the side street and said "all's well" as my car returned to the highway without incident, and I continued on my way. This happened in just a moment, with no time for me to stop for the intruding vehicle, but it had turned into slow motion as I drove my car with a sense of complete calm and the knowledge that all would be well.

Knowing, or kenning, is a vital part of what is usually called magic.

Curiously, some of those wandering physicists have now determined as possible what witches have always known: all time is the same time, and everything that has happened or will happen is happening simultaneously, meaning that time is not lineal but more like a spiral that you can access at different points to make changes. This sense of time also aligns with the concept of the Akashic Records, a place where all the information about everything that has been, is, and will be is stored, like a library, and can be accessed. This is why you can "play" with time. The average person will say "nonsense" or be horrified at the thought. Try not to panic, for when approached with the confidence that the Divine will not let you hurt yourself or other people (Perfect Love and Perfect Trust), you can make important changes. If there were a danger in taking any action, you would be alerted. Knowing, or kenning, is a vital part of what is usually called magic. This is not illusion (although it can be, as with glamour, covered in chapter 4) nor slight-of-hand like a stage performance but is the actual connecting with and moving of energy.

With this in mind, I must extrapolate on my mother's recitation of what I called the Rules of Conduct in the introduction and how those rules apply when engaged in any magical work, but especially in temporal manipulation. Being careful of what you do means you must consider the consequences of your actions before you launch into manifesting something. Being careful of who you trust reminds you to be circumspect with the people you confide in, for they might not be as trustworthy as you suppose.

Since what is sent comes back, using the Power for negative or harmful purposes can boomerang back onto you. My mother did not say "three-fold," as is common with Wicca today, only that there is balance and what is sent returns. The concept of balance is also an important aspect of Fairy connection and communication.

There are ways to alleviate the returning energy, and that is one of the secrets I am revealing here. When sending out negativity, you do so because you feel there is no other choice or at least you are not able to think of one. I highly recommend a meditative consultation or a simple inquiry with the Divine as to alternative options, and then listening to and acting on what you are told. With the former, you may engage in an astral encounter with someone who feels inclined to counsel you or with a spirit guide who offers advice. With the latter technique, you may hear a voice in your head speaking to you or you may have a vision. Above all, avoid placing yourself in a judgmental position, assuming that you know better than anyone else in this world (or any other) or the Divine.

If you do send out negative energy, you can mitigate the rebound energy by intentionally doing "good works" (such as donating food to a food bank) or by transferring the returning energy into an object that you are attached to. Putting it in mildly scientific terms, because you exchange molecules with everything, things that you possess, and those you especially like, will take on more of your energy and can be used to draw and contain returning negativity without doing you any harm. From the witch's perspective, objects hold on to the energy of those who use them frequently or are emotionally attached to them.

This is the basis of psychometry, the art of divination through holding or touching an object that belongs (or belonged) to someone else.

· · · · · · ·

Objects hold the energy of those who use them frequently or are emotionally attached to them.

For this use, the object has to be something you like in order for it to be a sacrifice that clears your own aura and your spiritual light. This clearing occurs only after you dispose of the object you were energetically attached to. You can put the object into the garbage (out of doors, not inside your home) to be taken away. If something small, like a piece of jewelry, you can bury it in a public area off your property, such as on the beach or in the woods. If someone finds it and takes it, no harm is done as the return energy is dissipated into the sand or ground as soon as buried. But do not then reclaim the object, for a sacrifice means giving something up, not taking it back. Since fire enlivens things (flame of life), I don't recommend burning such an object as that tends to send the wrong message. If using the garbage bin, envision the object as going from waste collection to a landfill where the energy will be transferred into the earth for cleansing and recycling.

This whole process is called transference magic. Transferring negative energy can also be used to protect those (and what) you care about. As you send the object away, you cut the energy cord between it and yourself by envisioning it as a stretched elastic string (or a tendril) between you and it, and with your hand or athame (a double-edged, usually black-handled ritual knife), slice through it and "see" the elastic/tendril whipping back to the object. Transference magic is also used when you hang a garlic or onion braid in the house to collect negative energies and dispose of it at the end of the year or when a plant is taken to a sick person to absorb the illness. As the plant withers, the person recovers. You must ask the plant's permission and receive it for this to work. Plants that agree to this arrangement may do so to increase their own spiritual light.

Sometimes negativity simply arrives unfocused. It may come from the land spirits, especially in locations where many people have died in battle or from illness, or more often from the unspoken ill will of other people, most of whom have no idea they are transmitting negative energy. This is generally called the evil eye and comes from such emotions as jealousy, envy, spite, or just bad temperament. When things are going badly or you feel there is a heaviness in the atmosphere, you can channel that energy into an object and cast it from your environment. The object acts as a lure, gathering the negativity to it, and once it is gone, things start to improve. The catch is that you have to like it for it to be an appropriate sacrifice. Be careful to focus your intention of moving the negative energy into the object, be it a piece of jewelry, a favorite art piece or craft, a piece of clothing, a dish, etc.

Most witches are very careful about clearing away their own connecting energy from anything they are giving away or putting out for a garage sale. An easy way to do this is by wafting sage smoke around the object with spoken words of clearing, such as:

> This smoke clears away my energy from this
> object. Through the Goddess and the God and
> the elementals Earth, Air, Fire, and Water,
> this object is cleared. So mote it be!

You may wash a small object in spring water (bottled is fine) and set it on a cluster of amethyst points to dry. You can add a muslin bag with lavender flowers to your laundry for clearing when you wash your clothes, towels, or tablecloths to remove attached energies. Placing an object in a bowl of salt or burying it in the dirt during a full moon or for three days will also clear away negativity, but not everything reacts well to these options. As a warning, do not place amethyst in the sunlight for clearing. Amethyst is a high-vibration stone that needs no clearing, and sunlight will fade the purple color. Read up about a stone before using it so you don't harm it.

The rule of never using the Power against a fellow practitioner is a reminder that we are all the children of the Divine, and sibling rivalry is just as ugly in energy work as in everyday life. Find another way to sort things out, end the relationship, or simply ignore and go your own way. With negativity directed toward others of the Craft, the option of transference magic may not work because you are sending your malice down the same channel you utilize. If someone in the Craft is offensive to you, withdraw from that person. If strife continues, set up protection energy or reversal energy around yourself, insulating yourself.

Another magical technique is called containment magic. Envision a clear glass or solid ceramic bowl upside down over the person or place that causes you problems, but leave it open at the bottom. This way the negativity cannot escape the aura of the person, but it can be grounded through the bottom into the earth for cleansing and recycling. If you close off the bottom of the upside-down bowl, the energy is trapped and the person or place will suffer, so remember the rule of "Harm None" and the rule of returning energy. There are other ways to handle in-house antagonisms, and if you are unable to come up with something yourself, ask the Divine for a solution. Put it in their capable hands.

How to Manipulate Time

The rule that to use the Power you must feel it and know it is vital for successful magical workings. This is both empathy and acknowledgment working harmoniously to create the heart-set and mind-set required to manifest the energy in physical reality. This combination creates the magical energy. If you are emotionally uncertain or mentally skeptical of what you are doing, you will fail or you will get strange or unexpected results from misguided magical energy. The importance of this last rule is the key to working with temporal magic. With our busy lifestyles and daily activities, it's possible that worries, anxieties, and stress may arise from the need to be on time, make it to appointments, or complete a project on a schedule. This can result in nervousness that may affect decision-making or create physical health problems, but Time can be your best friend.

As an ordinary example: if I am driving down the road and need to be somewhere by a certain time, and looking at the car clock tells me that I will most likely be late, I will either state aloud or think clearly, "I will arrive five minutes before _____ (the time when I need to arrive)." After that, I do NOT look at the clock again, and I do NOT think about the time again because I KNOW that I will arrive early to my destination. There is no doubting the outcome, nor are there any furtive glances at the clock nor any sense of urgency or concern. I drive normally and relaxed, traffic moves along normally, and I reach my destination five minutes early. It is as though a bubble of temporal energy envelopes the car and carries it along to achieve my goal while not interfering with anyone else.

When approaching a traffic light that is green, I may say "Stay green" until I am through the intersection. If the light is red, I may say something like "A little green would be nice about now." The light usually changes to green. If the traffic light does not stay green or turn green, I assume that the Universe is watching over me and there is a reason, so I enjoy the moment of pause with gratitude, knowing that all will be well. On one such event, stopping at the light for a couple of minutes prevented me from being in a location where a small truck was losing cargo out the back. On another occasion, I was able to see some unexpected wildlife, which I thoroughly enjoy. I also say things like "Time is my buddy." A bit of playfulness is much appreciated in the Universe.

Déjà Vu and How to Use It

Perhaps time is based more on our perception, which means we can slow it down or repeat events. A perfect example of understanding the spiral nature of time and manipulating it is the déjà vu experience. This is when, as you are experiencing something, you recognize *in that moment* that you have done this before. To me, whenever this happens, I feel that the Universe, the Divine, is offering me an opportunity to instantly evaluate how the experience played out before and how to now make a change. In one case I had a déjà vu that repeated five times, with me making subtle changes each time until I got it right. How to explain the looping of incidents is difficult at best. It seems to me that when you are trying to "fix" something that initially went wrong, the Divine, or the Universe, may be able to pull the event out of time and shift it to a future time or times, thus holding that event in abeyance and allowing you to keep tweaking that moment until the result is satisfactory and the event flows smoothly. As a result, when I was aware of that particular déjà vu at the time, I was also aware of each previous alteration that did not help matters, and I made a subtle change each time until the last one, which proved satisfactory.

- - - - - - -

Déjà vu allows you to keep tweaking the moment until the result is satisfactory.

Being alert to the sensation of repeated experience will allow you to immediately see the end result of your action or words in that moment so that you can change something. As an example of a simple déjà vu, I was sitting at dinner with my parents, brother, his fiancée, and a friend of mine from school, with lots of conversation and cross-table chatting going on. At the end of the meal, everyone got a slice of fresh cherry pie. My brother took a bite of his pie and gave a shout, then said angrily, "Of everyone here at the table, only *I* would bite down on a cherry pit!"

I instantly saw that my father would make a remark, my brother would respond, and I would say something silly that, although initially innocent, would incite a furious argument between my brother and father, ending with my brother and his fiancée departing the house in anger. Sure enough, my father made his remark and my brother made his, but I kept my mouth shut and clamped my teeth to keep from speaking, for I really wanted to make the wisecrack.

Suddenly all of the talk around the table stopped cold, and *everyone* turned their heads and looked right at me. I remained silent, people returned to their general chatting as though nothing had happened, and there was no argument or angry departure. Later my mother asked me what had happened at the table, and when I explained she smiled and nodded her approval. Working magically with temporal energy is so casual that most people are reluctant to accept this and overwork the process, thereby throwing up conditions and barricades when all you really need is to FEEL it as a subtle reality and to KNOW it as taken for granted in order to manifest what is desired.

chapter

2

Who and What
Are the Other People?

There are so many divergent concepts of the Other People and so many definitions and descriptions that books about Faerie are filled with the fairy types, their interactions with humans, the customs used to ward against them, and oral traditions of encounters both positive and negative. Each culture has its own names for the fairies, and each culture has its own rules and warnings about interaction, but the overall implication is that contact may be fraught with danger. Some books address so many fairy varieties that the list quickly becomes unmanageable, especially since most of the types have been reframed to conform to mainstream religious views. I do not accept this. They are what they are, and trying to encapsulate the Other People into a definition that minimalizes or cloaks them in derisive terms has to be offensive. Labeling one of the Other People as evil or malignant or destructive only invites that kind of response.

Appearances of the Other People

This is a dual-meaning heading, referring both to when they turn up and what they look like. If you enter the Otherworld with the expectation that all will be well, that is how it will go. If you enter with misgivings and uncertainties, things may not go as well as they could. The Other People have impeccable manners and will comply with what is expected. They will give to you what you seek. In other words, if you enter with trepidation, you will encounter situations and people that feed into that fear. In some ways, they are like a reflection of your mind-set and heart-set, so cultivate and remember Perfect Love and Perfect Trust. If you enter *knowing* (kenning) that you are among friends, you will be.

One of the most offensive terms for me, and certainly for the Other People, comes from a Scottish folk tradition that is now spreading into other cultures: that of the Seelie Court and the Unseelie Court, with the former being good and the latter being evil. *Seelie* is "blessed" or "holy," and *Unseelie* is "unblessed" or "unholy." The Unseelie Court seems to be mainly associated with the Wild Hunt, the Host, or the Rade. I feel the designation as unholy came into being as a way to disparage and demean the God in the form of the Hunter who leads it, since this could be any number of the old Pagan deities. The Hunt gathers the spirits of the dead to Underworld, and since these deities were rivals to the new spiritual worldview, they were labeled as "unblessed" or "unholy," demoted from deity status to fairy and then further labeled as evil. In this way, fear was created in the minds of the people to prevent them from retaining the old deities, but with this fear came a sense of being careful not to antagonize the old gods or insult them, lest they retaliate.

Spirits of the dead are also associated with the Other People, and I don't try to quibble about this. In fact, it may well be that the Summerland afterlife of Paganism is part of the Otherworld or connects with it through the Wild Hunt. I recounted the cherry pit incident a few decades later at a small gathering where I was guest speaker, and I told them that my brother was laughing about it in spirit next to me as I spoke (he had passed away fifteen years prior). I could see that most were skeptical. To prove my point, and with total confidence, I said that after my talk, I would eat a slice of the cherry pie I had seen on the buffet table and my brother would demonstrate his presence by making sure I got a cherry pit. Sure enough, and to the astonishment (or shock) of some of the guests, my slice contained a cherry with the pit still in it, which was a kind of balance for my brother and me.

The Other People may interact with humans, appearing to give a message or intercede in a kindly way, give a warning, prevent a person from desecrating their sacred territory, or in simply passing by. They may appear as humans or take on the form of an animal, inhabit a plant, or even momentarily "step into" another human, usually when there is dire need, as a need for self-defense (fighting off an attacker) or to achieve a feat of strength (lifting a car off a person), for the Other People are both formidable warriors and immensely strong. Scientists say that the dumping of adrenaline and cortisol into the bloodstream, onto the heart, and into the muscles is what creates the ability for superhuman achievements, but the actual source for this is not clearly addressed, with stress being considered the prime motivator.

If you enter the Otherworld with the expectation that all will be well, that is how it will go.

Whether the Other People are solid beings, spirits, or amorphous entities able to shift into any form or enter any object is a matter of speculation. Coming into contact with them creates in most humans a definite sensation of brushing up against something out of the ordinary, something uncanny. This is not necessarily a bad thing, as it alerts a person to be on their best behavior. When given a message, it is best to pay attention.

Just like humans, the Other People vary in size and shape, but their "presence" is always an indicator of their true nature. I once had a solid black cat with three white hairs on his chest. He was a wonderful companion with an aura of wisdom. When someone took a Polaroid photo of a child kneeling next to him, the child was clearly visible, but the cat was simply a blaze of pure white light. One day I was browsing through Katharine Briggs's *Encyclopedia of Fairies* and found that he matched the description of a Fairy Cat, which felt appropriate to me. Cats are sacred to the Goddess, and black cats in particular have been considered to be the helpers (familiars) of witches. During the European Middle Ages, cats in general were killed as minions of the Devil.

Fairies might show up unexpectedly, being helpful, just passing through, or sometimes they are simply looking for a friend.

You cannot judge fairies by definitions placed upon them by people who have their own agenda.

I taught a class demonstrating how I conduct a sabbat ritual so the students could take notes and later plan together their own class ritual for an upcoming sabbat. One of the students was a child of ten or eleven, accompanied by a parent who was also a student. I demonstrated sweeping the circle with my ritual broom, saying as I went around the group sitting on the floor, "Let the besom clear away any negative or chaotic energies," when there appeared a tiny greenish light that quickly took the form of small sprite next to the child. The sprite put its hands together in a pleading motion, looking up at me while silently asking to be allowed to remain, so I paused and inserted into my statement, "...except for this one..." and continued the circle casting as normal. The sprite's expression of utter joy made me feel confident that I had done the right thing.

Throughout the class lesson, I would catch a glimpse of the little sprite sitting tranquilly next to the child. Later, with everyone standing, I demonstrated the ritual, and when I began the Cakes and Wine part, putting the athame blade into the chalice, an adult in the class blurted out, "Oh boy! Pagan sex!" I ignored the remark, continuing without pause, but I noticed the person was now quiet and remained so for the rest of the class. After the other students had left, the offending student came up to me and apologized for the uncontrolled remark, blaming it on excitement and telling me that after saying it, a bright green light had zoomed up from the floor to right between the person's eyes and shouted, "I'm being good, why aren't you!!"—and after that the student couldn't speak. The real point of this episode is that you cannot judge the fairies by definitions placed on them by people who have their own perspective or agenda. Although an otherwise mischievous sprite felt it could be swept from the circle, it promised to behave in order to remain with the child for class. The sprite then silenced someone whose behavior was inappropriate and who was not allowed to speak again until the child and sprite had departed. Even the smallest of the Other People have power.

When it comes to the Other People, I try not to create categories, especially since there appears to be a fluid transition between this world and the Otherworld. To me there is no need to get too picky about creating boundaries where there might not actually be any. I cannot separate devas (the life-force entities of Nature), spirits of Nature, or spirits of the land from fairies. A good example of the flexible boundaries of definitions between mound dwellers and plant spirits is the blackthorn shrub. These are sturdy, thorny plants sacred in Paganism since ancient times, with their white flowers blooming in March prior to the plant leafing out. In the British Isles, blackthorn bushes are said to be inhabited by fairies called the Lunantishee, usually described as particularly malevolent fairies or as guardians of the blackthorn who punish anyone that cuts the wood on Samhain or Beltane of the Julian calendar (of Julius Caesar), today's Old November Eve (November 11) and Old May Eve (May 11). Since the blackthorn was associated with the staffs or walking sticks of the wise men and women of the Old Religion—the healers, spellcasters, and diviners—people were discouraged from using what became labeled as a baneful wood from the period of cultural change to the present, but it also shows the Lunantishee as an in-dwelling nature spirit associated with the traditional mound dwellers.

Not only are there numerous types of Other People who fit under the umbrella of fairy, there is also a large variety of Other People who are called elves. In the case of the elves (or álfar), as related by Icelandic historian Snorri Sturluson in his *Prose Edda* of the thirteenth century, they are collectively called the Vanir, dwelling in Vanaheim (one of the Nine Worlds of Norse tradition). The elves are deities of Nature, the sea, the land, fertility, life, death, and magic, and are divided into the three main branches: light elves (*ljósálfar*), dark elves (*dokkálfar*), and swarthy (black/shadow) elves (*svartálfar*). The light elves live in Álfheim (Elf-Home) under the rulership of the Vanir god Freyr, and they are subdivided into mountain elves (*muntælfen*), land/field elves (*landælfen*), water/river elves (*wæterælfen*), sea elves (*saeælfen*), and wood elves (*wuduælfen*). The dark or swarthy elves lived in Svartalfheim (Swarthy-Elf-Home) and were blacksmiths and miners respectively (not to be confused with dwarves, who had their own world called Nidavellir). Some of this may look familiar as a source for the world of J. R. R. Tolkien's Lord of the Rings trilogy, but it also points out that there are categories of elves and possibly a large number of subcategories, all of whom may be contacted for assistance and honored with offerings. I only mention the delineations, but I do not get too wrapped up with these definitions simply because some of them overlap depending on the source, and who comes to visit is not always scripted.

Selkies are seal-people, thus a variety of sea elves, as are undines, mermaids, and mermen. The selkies shed their seal skins now and then, and by finding one and stealing it, a human can gain a spouse until such time as the selkie regains the skin and goes back to the sea. Pookas are fairies that appear as sleek horses with long wild manes and the power of speech. They are described in contradictory terms, depending on the location and regional custom, as being mischievous, dangerous, or helpful. They are considered to be nature spirits and are generally benevolent. As shapeshifters, they can appear as a variety of animals such as a horse, rabbit, cat, dog, wolf, fox, bull, goat, and so on, and they are able to talk and help or hinder humans. Several fairy tales involve talking animals, such as the fox in "The Water of Life" and the horse head in "The Goose Girl."

Cultural traditions vary concerning fairy dogs, making them usually something to be avoided. The white hounds with red-tipped ears are supposed to accompany Death; black dogs, especially those with red eyes, are considered evil; and white ones as not particularly malevolent; all should be avoided because they are connected with Otherworld. White horses are suspect, but black horses are considered evil and murderous. Clothing colors are associated with "good" or "bad" Other Folk, with red and black seen as dangerous or malefic and red caps particularly murderous. Gray is unpredictable, while green indicates a being that is Nature oriented. Just working with the Other People or communicating with spirits and nature entities is sufficient to evoke fear and distrust in people due to the mainstream social atmosphere. Certainly, be careful with whom you discuss such matters, but also recognize that your own fears or superstitions may be culturally influenced. Likewise, unusual physical features occur in the natural world; I have seen a two-headed calf and a five-legged lamb, but that does not make them evil.

Recognize that your own fears or superstitions may be culturally influenced.

One thing to keep in mind about spirit guides is that you should not expect them to answer all your questions or give you explanations, even in lucid dreams, visions, or meditations. They may not be as instructional as you would like, but they may watch over you as you deal with the challenges of this life. Guides can know the various alternatives that your actions may create, rather like looking at the threads of a tapestry where the pattern is in progress, but they rarely intervene to tell you which path to choose. Sometimes it is not about us, but we are merely a cog in the greater wheel of universal experience. Besides not answering your questions, guides may withhold information, and you should trust your guide's decision and let things evolve as intended by the Universe.

Once you begin to communicate with the Other People, they might decide to help you without your asking. I was dusting furniture at home and was nearly done when the phone rang. I went to answer it and chatted a little before returning to work on the one corner table left unfinished. As I approached the living room, a very hairy little person, about four feet tall, darted out of the room, into the entry hall, and vanished into thin air. I went on in to continue dusting (I tend to take this sort of thing in stride), but the table and everything on it was already clean. I was now certain that I had seen a grogan, a short, hairy fairy that will help with chores and may be attached to the person or to the land.

Rosemary by the door to the house lets the Other People know they are welcome at my home.

Another time at a house where the kitchen opened to the family room and backyard, I was washing dishes and saw over the counter the tops of the heads of what looked to be three golden-haired children walking quickly past the counter toward the back door. I expected to see them come into sight from the end of the counter, but they vanished. Since my backyard had a large herb garden and a variety of trees as well as a wild space, I was not surprised they were headed out that way.

I grew up with the custom of leaving milk out for the Fair Folk at the full moon. I grow rosemary by the door to the house, and this lets the Other People know that they are welcome at my home. The cleansing scent of lavender is another way of attracting the Other People. The color green is associated with the Other People, elves, the Lord and Lady of Nature, and the elementals collectively. When the color was used in medieval stories and songs, it was an indicator as to the true nature of a character as Other, such as in the medieval song of Lady Greensleeves and the tale of the Green Knight in the Arthurian stories. Historically, only people who were in kinship or affinity with the Fair Ones wore green clothing, and there were strict rules in the making of green dyes, among them being that in some regions, men were forbidden to take part in the process. For the ordinary person, green was considered an "unlucky" color, although there is less of that notion today. I remember as a child hearing people say that green was an unlucky color for a car or a house, but now greens are much more common. Using green colors for home décor inside or out, for clothing, or for vehicles is another signal to the Other People that you are friendly.

Seeing and Communicating with Dragons

Dragons have a mixed history with humans, being described as wise, a vehicle for divine beings to ride, or rampaging killers who destroy villages with fire and eat cattle, sheep, and humans. In the Chinese tradition, dragons are revered and are generally seen as long, slender, snakelike beings with feet who are able to fly through the skies. In the Hindu tradition, the god Vishnu rides the Garuda, a winged creature who looks like a human with a birdlike head and eagle-like beak but might also be depicted as a dragon. The Aztecs and Mayans revered a flying feathered serpent that in art and architecture looks like a dragon. In some descriptions dragons are called worms, which emphasizes the serpent appearance. Medieval artwork depicting the garden of Eden often showed Eve being tempted by a snakelike creature with a human face, remarkably similar to the depictions of the feathered serpents of the Mayans and the Aztecs, called Kukulkan and Quetzalcoatl respectively. Dragons are described as wise and good or as conniving and evil.

I had not actually thought of dragons as dwelling in Otherworld until I did a meditation with my spirit guide horse and encountered a group of dragons within a sidhe inhabited by a lively crowd of glittering, opulently attired Other People at a banquet. There was a king, it seemed to me, sitting casually on a dais apart from the crowd and looking a little bored or perhaps he had something on his mind. I chatted with the elegant folk about some assistance I sought at the time, and they were enthusiastic and cheerful but suggested that the dragons might perhaps be more helpful. That was when my horse nudged me (she had led me past the guard and into the banquet hall), and I spotted dimly visible shadows moving in the darkened far corner of the room and realized there were dragons inside the sidhe.

If you desire to work with dragons, be aware that they are exacting. When asked to assist me with a project, they agreed but gave me a condition. I readily accepted it, but after a time, I let it go. That resulted in physical depletion, and I understood at once that I had violated the condition and the dragons stopped helping me. This is where making amends comes in. When you mess up, and it happens, acknowledge your error and release the connection. I spoke aloud to the dragons my apology and told them that I knew at the time I would probably not be able to live up to the condition required, but I had desired their help so much that I was careless. This admission released my end of the agreement. I next stated that I took full responsibility for my actions and understood that the agreement between us was null and void, yet I would be very grateful for their continued friendship and counsel.

> *When you mess up, and it happens, acknowledge your error and release the connection.*

This acknowledgment released them from their end of the agreement. When something like this happens, you have to sever *both* ends of the energy connection to bring closure and restore balance. I severed the agreement by violating the condition, but the deleterious results would have remained until the agreement was voided on my end by the apology and on their end by my taking responsibility for the error. Cutting the energy cords brought balance and allowed us to return to our original state. Dragons have continued to drop in on me from time to time, and I am quite happy that I eventually found my own way to achieve my goal.

I have had several encounters with dragons, and mostly they appear as large four-footed creatures with long tails who can sit upright and use their front feet as hands. The ones I have met had scales and fangs, although wings were not always readily in view. I have not gone to them so much as they have arrived where I am. The first dragon that came to me was a green one who gave me this advice: "When speaking with dragons, do not grovel or be humble, lest the dragon feel demeaned for having thought better of you." That was an unusual understanding of communication for me, but it let me know their perspective when it came to contacting humans and kept me from being intimidated by the sheer size and power of the dragon. I felt confident enough to ask that one if I could touch a scale to understand the texture, and I was allowed to do so.

Dragons come in different colors, relating to their energies. The ones I am familiar with are green dragons oriented to land, blue dragons to water, golden to solar, white to air, red to fire, silver to lunar, black to shadow, and crystal to ascension. To work with dragons, you need a heart-set of friendship and a mind-set of confidence. I once did a clearing of my chakras (the spinning energy vortexes of the body) and at one of the chakras, a glittering coal-black horned dragon with upraised wings appeared, looking fierce, aggressive, and menacing. I focused on what that chakra represented and my life experiences that related to that chakra, then released the negative energy associated with that energy vortex, cutting the cord with a blessing. Instantly the black dragon turned into a radiant crystal dragon, then vanished, and I continued clearing chakras.

To do this meditation, stand and cast a circle around yourself. Place a bowl of salt at the north, light incense at the east, light a white candle at the south, and set a bowl of water at the west. Sit at the center of the circle and use a crystal point or wand to clear each chakra. This is not a quick process. It requires you to point the crystal at the chakras one at a time, asking to see what needs to be cleared: "Show me what blockages need clearing." Go back into your lifetime memories and think about how that energy center may have been affected by past negative events, then give the memories a blessing and release them. There might be only one energy center or several out of balance or otherwise impaired.

When recalling the negative event to mind, explore the possibilities of the surrounding circumstances within the security of your circle, consider the perspective of others involved and the influences that may have shaped them, and then realize that you do not need to be restricted by the past, but instead offer forgiveness and blessing, then release it. See yourself severing the energy cord connecting you to this event with a motion of your hand as though a knife is cutting a cord, and see the cord whisk away and vanish like a snap of elastic. You have only severed your end of the energy cord; now it is no longer your concern but is up to whatever lies at the other end to handle. Sometimes people hold onto negative memories without realizing that others who may have participated in that memory have long forgotten about it, were unaware of any harm done, or simply didn't care. That is no longer an issue you need to deal with or continue to mull over, for it is released and you are liberated. I recommend taking a box of tissues with you in the circle before casting because the process can stir up the emotions.

There are different ways to connect with dragons. They can be encountered in meditation, astral projection, lucid dreams, portals, clouds, or visions. Clouds may normally appear as ordinary and nondescript until a message needs to be sent or an opportunity is revealed for a desire to be granted. When that happens, the clouds you see will take on shapes or forms. By recognizing the association, you can then speak with Otherworld beings.

I believe that clouds can provide an intersection between the worlds just as portal stones and black mirrors do, so seeing things in the clouds may be much more than simple pareidolia (organizing vague images into recognizable patterns). The term is also an example of science creating a definition for an experience which, if accepted, diminishes its significance to the recipient, thus bringing the person into conformity with the socially established standard.

Clouds are an easy way of accessing dragons. I have seen dragons in the clouds, greeted them, and received answers to questions or helpful responses to my requests. I once received reassurance that this kind of contact is real when I saw a white, feathery, serpent-like dragon in the clouds and after greeting it, the dragon sent a mental message to me. The feathery dragon melted away and a new dragon appeared, looking like a Garuda. I had never seen one before and I was delighted to see it. I offered it a respectful blessing and asked for one in return, which it gave to me, then melted away.

Later that day, a shamanic healer arrived at my shop and told me about seeing two dragons in the clouds while on the way over to do energy work, and when greeted, each offered an important message. The shaman said one was a white, feathery serpent undulating in the sky and the other was a Garuda, so this gave confirmation that what I had seen were not mere shapes in the clouds, but visions through a temporary portal that opened and closed for me, then opened and closed later on for the shaman long after I had seen them.

· · · · · · ·

If you desire to meet a dragon and one appears to you, fleeing is not considered good manners.

You can let dragons know you are interested in communication by growing plants that relate to dragons (such as snapdragons, dragon trees, or dragon fruit cactus), having dragon images (jewelry, figu-rines, or pictures), or engaging in activities or shaping your surroundings with a focus on the type of dragon and element associated with it: garden for green, water feature for blue, fire pit for red, sun disk for gold, moon disk/crescent for silver, wind chimes or outdoor streamers for white, etc. Use your intuition as to what will appeal to you and to them. Dragons may shapeshift or enter this world in a human form, but they will have a certain quality about them that may feel Otherworldly to you. If you desire to meet a dragon and one appears to you, fleeing is not considered good manners. Dragons are also very particular about the more subtle meanings of words, which makes conversation more penetrating than usual, so be especially courteous when speaking with them and choose your words with care.

Seeing and Communicating with Unicorns

Unicorns are more likely to be seen by young children who have open minds and hearts unhindered by parental or societal restrictions. Usually dismissed as imaginary, these encounters may in fact be quite real. I acknowledge that my connection with unicorns has been limited, although I am aware of people whose interactions have been profound. I am more likely to encounter these amazing creatures in deep meditation, clouds, or through proximity to someone who has an easy association with them. The child mentioned earlier who vanished while romping with the unicorns and then reappeared soon after was initially playing with a plush stand-up unicorn toy in a large mowed grassy backyard, so the parent's view was unhindered. This child also used the unicorn toy as a guardian and would set the toy so it faced the bedroom door at night, preventing any intrusion. The parent sensed the unicorn's purpose and would not even clean in that room without the child being present to approve.

The only colors I am aware of for unicorns are white and black. The white unicorns tend to be gentle, with wisdom to share and strength to provide protection and assistance. The black unicorns tend to be a rougher crowd but probably one you would be happy to have on your side in any difficult situation. They can be approached for assistance if you are bold enough to seek them out, although they are unlikely to tolerate any amount of impertinence. I once saw roiling black clouds moving swiftly across the sky and I could discern within it a herd of black unicorns racing with wild abandon toward the area where I lived. I and the person with me called aloud to the white unicorns to come and turn aside the rampaging herd so as not to cause harm where people dwelled, and we were happily amazed to see puffy white clouds race into view in which we could see white unicorns, who pushed against the black unicorns and turned them away from habitations.

I feel that the energies of Nature, such as in an impending storm, are stirred into creating a channel between worlds or dimensions, and that by reading, seeing, or interpreting things in the clouds, you become the recipient of information so you are able to interact with beings or powers from these other worlds to affect things in this world. The color of the black unicorns may indicate a connection with the Wild Hunt, while the white unicorns may suggest a benevolent energy, and just as with the Wild Hunt, you will note where the herd is going and either avoid that location or call for a more positive energy to avert potential disaster.

Unicorns are fierce defenders of those to whom they attune, particularly children. That horn is not for decoration but is a powerful weapon both magically and physically. Although usually depicted as horses with a horn in the center of their foreheads, they are actually not equine but are unique creatures of Otherworld. The ones I have seen in meditation, portals, or in the clouds are graceful, sleek, and powerful, with a body shape resembling a slender deer, hooves (I've never noticed cloven hooves), a central spiral horn just above the eyes, long shaggy mane and fetlocks, lionlike tail, and goatlike beard.

Protectors and Observers

The child's toy unicorn is also an example of an in-dwelling spirit. Plushy toys and dolls are most likely to be used by children for comfort and protection when they feel alone or frightened. So-called haunted dolls and other such toys have most likely retained the energy called into it by the child that named it, played with it, and saw it as alive or *real*. Even years later, a stranger may feel that energy and declare that the object is creepy or haunted. When you grow up and put aside or dispose of old toys, remember to release any spirit attachment with gratitude for the companionship and a blessing so the transition is a gentle one. Sometimes the in-dwelling spirit will move on, but other times such a spirit will remain around the person as a guardian. Adults can also use objects, such as a vehicle, to play host to an in-dwelling spirit. Remembering that Spirit is in everything and that everything is therefore alive makes this more understandable. The spirits who enter objects do so willingly, perhaps as loved ones from past lives, ancestors of a person's bloodline, or to increase their spiritual light through protection activity. It is also possible that a spirit may use this type of activity as a way to work off karma from past life misdeeds.

Children are able to visualize their toys talking to them or otherwise being real. If you can cultivate this talent and hold onto it, you will have the essence of bringing life to your important objects. Many people think of their vehicle as having a personality, be it a car, van, truck, bicycle, motorcycle, etc. As a child, I named my bicycle and knew it would keep me safe no matter where I pedaled it. People who give their cars or other transportation vehicles names are basically calling in a helpful spirit to be a protective or supportive presence. The more energy a person, young or old, puts into an object, the more this will attract a compatible spirit. As an adult, I named my first car and trusted it to keep me safe no matter where I drove it, and it did. This is a way of bringing a helpful spirit into an otherwise "inanimate" object for protection and companionship. You don't have to consciously call someone into the object, but simply talking to it and seeing it as your buddy will draw in the spirit you need. To make this a successful endeavor, you have to be just as fully engaged as a child, not analytical, aloof, self-conscious, or doubtful.

Stuffed plushy animals make a good host for a spirit to in-dwell. When I see vehicles with stuffed animal toys or dolls in a window or on the car seat, I know these may be protectors brought in by the owner, whether deliberately or intuitively. When done deliberately, you can give the plushy in your car instructions to protect against intruders or accidents. But you have to *know* that the plushy or whatever object you use for this will do the job assigned. I was delighted when a magic practitioner I know once confided to me that when leaving the car, a plushy toy is directed to keep it safe. I do something similar with a couple of plushies in my car, and they know what their jobs are and fulfill their duties quite well.

There is another type of in-dwelling spirit activation for deity statues, called a consecration,[3] in which you ask for a bit of the Infinite Spirit of the Divine to enter into the statue. When you meditate or ask for assistance or place offerings in front of the image, you are not worshipping it any more than you would worship a telephone. You are connecting with the Divine through the symbol that you have asked the Divine to enter for presence and contact. The offering is your way of refreshing that connection or of expressing your gratitude for assistance rendered. My method may differ from yours, but if you are satisfied with the result, then that is all that matters. I have had students do the Consecration of a Statue ritual in class, and they are amazed at the difference before and after, with students even saying that their statues had come to life. What they were seeing was how a tiny portion of Divine Spirit entering into an image provides a focal point for the individual to readily communicate with the Goddess and the God.

Observers are nature spirits who are usually silent sentinels in a sacred space, whose presence is felt as a sense of power and peace, affording protection to those who dwell respectfully therein. Many cultures have sacred mountains, wells, springs, rocks, and caverns, to name a few types of sacred space, and here people go to reconnect with Nature, meditate, walk, and release worries or allow the activity and surroundings to generate answers to questions or solutions to problems. Breathing in the moist air of the forest, the dry air of the desert, or the crisp air of the mountains clears the mind and quiets the daily thought patterns to be sublimated by subconscious awareness. When you do this, all of Nature is tuning in and becoming accessible. People go to special water features such as falls, springs, and wells to feel the cleansing energy and perhaps sip or bathe in the healing waters. Others prefer to feel the energy of mountains, rocks, and boulders.

---

3 See *Grimoire for the Green Witch*.

When your mind is relaxed, your spirit is open to receive the healing, inspiration, or information needed. It is through that calmness the influence of the Observers in Nature may be felt and new awareness or their guidance may be received. While you may address the power of a sacred site or a location where you feel close to the energies of Nature, do not expect to have all your questions answered or all your needs addressed. You must walk your own path and live your own life, but an Observer may stand by you to point the best route to take. Still, it is always your choice whether or not to pay attention and trust your feelings. In modern society, intuition is not normally given credence, so it may take practice to embrace this natural ability.

When your mind is relaxed, your spirit is open to receive the healing or inspiration needed.

Sometimes the Observers will draw your attention to some object that will act as a reminder of your experience, be it a leaf, a nut, a pebble, or other natural item. This object is something you should treasure by placing it in a special location such as a personal shrine or altar area in your home or keeping it close to your person in a pouch or medicine bag. Just be sure you are not violating any laws prohibiting taking certain things, such as eagle feathers unless you are Native American or objects from a designated area such as national parks.

Most people can sense the presence of an Observer of Nature, and to some this indicates the presence of a deity such as the Master of the Wood, the Lord and Lady of Nature, or the presence of fairies and sprites. It could also be that the presence felt is that of the spirits of the trees, stones, and so on. Simply by acknowledging the presence and speaking to it, you establish a respectful greeting that shows your willingness to communicate. I once found a beautiful little bowl formed by a seed pod and commented aloud how much it delighted me and that I would like to use it on my altar at home, but I really needed two pods for this to be balanced. Another pod appeared nearby. My companions agreed that the pods made perfect containers for the altar and each asked for a pair as well, and as we took a few more steps, two sets of pods were on the path for them. Each of us gave a gift in return: shiny coins and spring water placed in a stone's indentation.

Life-Force Entities of Nature and Nature Spirits

The problem most people have with Faerie and the Other People is that of socially and culturally ingrained disbelief. If you have an experience and reveal this to someone, the person's likely response will be a number of scenarios intended to explain away the experience as not what you think it was. If you turn aside one suggestion, another one will be offered, and this may continue until you capitulate and agree that it did not happen as you thought it did. This kind of programming begins at childhood with parents not believing what the child tells them, then offering alternative interpretations until the child is silenced: you dreamt it, you imagined it, stop telling stories, go to your room, etc. It is not always that the parents really don't believe a child, but that they know this is unacceptable in society and are trying to stifle the spreading of this information to protect the child from being ostracized. Sometimes it is fear of the experience itself that drives parents to deny what their child tells them. Denial is reinforced as often as necessary to block a child's ability to experience Otherworld contact and program the child's mind into releasing this talent. Once a person has gone through this process, which is usually considered good parenting by society, the child is taught that whatever the senses say is unreliable because these things just don't happen, and—more than that—it is wrong and harmful to have such an encounter or believe it happened.

When people as adults start having contact with spirits, fairies, and more, they tend to feel there is nowhere to turn and no one with whom they can compare notes without being judged. I have been fortunate to have had numerous people tell me what a relief it is to be able to talk about these things with someone who has an open mind and who can offer suggestions. People do need to be careful about talking to folks about spirits, entities, fairies, dragons, and so on lest they be labeled unhinged and in need of medication or confinement. This is simply the reality of the world in which we live. So-called paranormal experiences are the stuff of "golly gee whiz" entertainment, not reality as society has been conditioned to define it.

There are a vast variety of Other People, including sprites, elves, nature spirits, and more in all of their subgroups. I have seen fairies in flowers and dryads in trees, and sometimes the plants are a venue for passing fairies to take a glimpse into our world, rather than being the spirit of the plant. In such a case, they come to see you or be seen, then dash off again, and the plant returns to a more normal appearance. Trolls are usually depicted as evil monsters, but in Scandinavian countries and Japan they are benign nature spirits. The Japanese anime film *My Neighbor Totoro* is about children who are excited to meet a troll (Totoro), who in turn helps them in their time of need (you need to watch the credits to see further developments through the still pictures placed in between).

· · · · · · ·

Sometimes plants are a venue for passing fairies to take a glimpse into our world.

Magic is really all about energy: working with energy, moving energy, opening gateways and portals, and closing them again. Energy is neither good nor bad; it is simply energy. Your perspective of how it impacts your life is what creates the good/bad identification. If you put aside the dichotomy outlook toward energy, you can influence it to work for you. That is one of the benefits of divination techniques such as reading tarot cards: you can see how the energies are lined up at present and (depending on the spread used) as much as six months into the future (remembering that all time is one time) and with this knowledge, you can make changes. It is unwise to try a lifetime reading simply because energy is always in motion and many of your viewpoints may alter or completely change over time. You can also deliberately change the energy flow to something you find more favorable simply by using words alone, as with positive affirmations, for words also have energy. For further reinforcement, you can burn a candle that you charge (energize by holding it in your hands) and state the purpose for which you are lighting it:

> *This candle is consecrated and charged through*
> *the power of the Divine and the elementals*
> *Earth, Air, Fire, and Water to _____*
> *(state the purpose of the candle). So mote it be.*

There are candles prepared by reputable companies that are energized for particular influences such as healing, spirit contact, removing blockages, bringing good fortune, and so on. Most can be found in metaphysical shops or even online, but as many are jar candles with herbs and oils added to them, damage in shipment may occur, so it may be best to create your own.

For better focus, you can choose a candle whose color matches the energy of what you seek to accomplish, then add your own herbs or oils (or both) to draw on their energies to enhance your purpose. Some people rub the oil on the outside of a candle and roll it in the herbs. I like to use jar candles that I "dress" by using a chopstick to make one to four holes in the wax, into which I can insert the appropriate essential oils by using a dropper. I then add one to four herbs to the candle, calling upon the particular energy within each that aligns with my goal. With jar candles, runic, planetary, or other symbols whose energies supplement or augment your intent can be inscribed on the top of the candle or on the jar itself with a marker.

Once you open yourself up to energy work, you may start seeing and feeling more spirit energy in the natural world around you. A plant has spirit and personality that becomes more accessible with more contact. I once grew mugwort in my herb garden, and I annually created a circle with a long shoot of it as a charm for the yard. One year the plant died after a frost, but then the remaining short stump sprouted one long leafy tendril in spring. I asked the mugwort if I could take that tendril to demonstrate how to make a circle for a planned workshop that day, and the plant literally screamed at me "NO!" I was quite shocked by the reaction and soothingly said okay, then the plant continued in a nervous tone, "You'll kill me." Now, this is not something I created in my mind or imagination, because honestly, why would I expect a plant to shout at me like that and follow it up with a more temperate explanation? I told the mugwort I would leave it alone and I instead asked if honeysuckle or jasmine would let me have a tendril for my class. Each abundant plant happily offered me lengthy sprigs.

Several weeks later I was in the garden and heard a distinct high-pitched call that sounded like "*Whee-you!*" It repeated again and I realized it came from the area where the mugwort was located. Going to see it, I was surprised to find that the plant was now huge, bushy, and shimmering. "You can have a sprig now!" the plant said cheerfully. I patted the mugwort and admired aloud how good it looked, then asked which sprig I could have. I saw the one indicated and used it for a circle to hang in one of the trees in the yard. Again, there was no reason for me to imagine this scenario as it had been weeks since I had even been in that area of the garden.

With the mugwort episode, there are several things to note: plants can and will talk to you, they can and will let you harvest portions of themselves and indicate which part by giving it a brighter appearance or sudden motion, and if a plant unexpectantly offers you a portion, you must accept, for to do otherwise is to insult the spirit of the plant. Beyond that, the plant spirit may be influenced by a fairy who sees that the time will come when you will require the herbal benefit of that plant. When taking a gift from a plant, be sure to give a gift. My mother always gave crushed eggshells, and I sometimes augment that with blessed water (not salted, just water I have blessed in the moonlight and stored for use) or a silver coin. Additionally, I talk to my plants. I praise them, I hold their blossoms in my hands and tell them how beautiful they are or how fragrant, and I caress them in the direction the branches grow. Experiments have been conducted that show how talking kindly to plants makes them feel secure so they flourish, while angry speech or threatening with fire makes them fearful and they grow stunted or wither. Witches have always known that kindly words are encouraging and harsh tones are discouraging, no matter to whom or what you are speaking.

When weeding, I will toss the weeds, roots and all, into a wild part of the yard where I tell them they can take root and grow happily. Burdock is a little trickster who likes to hide behind larger plants, but when spotted giggles mischievously. By pulling it up carefully and tossing it into the wild area, a flourishing patch of burdock flowers soon developed, which is lovely but also magically beneficial for protection and warding negativity.

Burdock is a little trickster who likes to hide behind larger plants, but when spotted giggles mischievously.

Insects are also responsive to heartfelt interaction. When weeding a mound near where I had shrubs and a little pond, I pulled up a large clump and from the hole came a mass of fire ants. I felt their panic and saw some grabbing the baby eggs and the defenders rushing to attack me, the dangerous intruder. I quickly apologized and set the clump back in place. I said aloud that I would leave the area covered for them to be safe and backed away from the mound. One fire ant latched onto my bare toe (I was wearing sandals), and I carefully picked it off, held it up to eye level, and told it not to worry, I meant them no harm. I set the fire ant back on the mound and it disappeared in the foliage. Surprisingly, my toe did not have the burning, itching reaction caused by a fire ant bite, and from then on, fire ants have not bothered me. Heart-set and mind-set includes recognizing that other creatures have feelings and fears, and by letting your energy expand toward them in love and understanding, you can allay their worries.

When communicating with anything in daily life, be it an animal or plant or even furniture, speak from the heart. The heart is the center from which love may be expanded outward for a positive connection. When I was a teenager on a family vacation, my father took a wrong turn on what he thought was a shortcut and we ended up deep in the forest on an isolated dirt road at dusk when the car broke down. It was a long hike back to the main paved road, and on the way I saw two foxes slinking alongside the dirt road, watching us intently. I felt their concern and I felt compassion for them as I said, "It's okay, we're not interested in your den and babies." Immediately the two foxes paused, then turned around and hurried back the way they came. A little later, as we hiked up a rise in the road, I saw a wolf on the hill, watching us from the middle of the road. My father was distracted by helping my mother with her heavy purse, but I felt joy at seeing the wolf, and it trotted off into the forest, leaving us undisturbed. We continued to the deserted main road with no further incident and, feeling confident that we would be fine, I was not surprised when a car appeared in the night and gave us a lift into town. Once there, we were taken in by a local family, and the next day they took us to a mechanic, who handled the problem so we were again on our way, on the correct road.

When communicating with anything in daily life, speak from the heart.

I was invited to a sister circle of some twenty women guided by a Native American wise woman and midwife who led the group in readings from *The 13 Original Clan Mothers* by Jamie Sams (of French, Cherokee, Seneca, and Mohawk descent) for a foundation in Native American traditions. In a naming activity, a beautifully decorated talking stick was passed around the circle and people were supposed to mentally hear their new name. I fully expected to simply hold the decorated stick for a moment, then pass it along, as I had not attended any of the previous meetings and was only a guest, but the moment I took hold of the stick, I was astonished and delighted to hear a very distinct voice speak a complete sentence, pause, and give me a new name, which I cherish to this day. I have two books written by Jamie Sams in which she uses the terms Grandfather or Grandmother as titles for the Sun and Moon, and this resonates with me since in Witchcraft these titles are used to designate a Craft Elder, as are the titles Granny, Grandpa, Mama, and Papa. By addressing an animal or plant with these titles, you are not simply speaking to the individual, but to that portion of Divine Spirit inherent in the species containing the complete information of that species and disseminated throughout the rest, which responds to you through the one you address.

Once I was driving on a country road and noticed a vulture standing on a post near roadkill. I initially felt repulsed but quickly realized this could be an opportunity to learn, so I asked aloud, "Grandfather Vulture, what is the truth of your people?" Immediately I received this answer: "I teach my children to eat the dead, and when I am dead, my children will eat me." This was the vulture view of the Circle of Life, their place within the ecosystem of our Mother Earth, and I greet them now with appreciation for their work. I later verified that vultures do indeed eat their own dead. You do not need to be in a meditative state to communicate, but you do need to be sincerely open to receiving a response.

Whenever I see roadkill, I offer a blessing to the spirit of the animal. On one such occasion I saw that the dead wild creature was a beautiful, fluffy red fox and I felt great sadness for this loss and also pity for the fox cut short in its prime of life. I blessed the fox and by a slight astral projection stroked the dead animal, feeling the soft fur under my fingers. Immediately I got a response: "I am NOT a pet!" and I felt the animal's spirit close by, demanding the respect of what it was from its perspective, not mine. I quickly apologized and let it know that I appreciated the life lesson it had given me, for I recognized now that it was an adult wild animal, proudly self-sufficient and not in need of any human caretaker. It seemed mollified by that and slightly surprised that I got the message. I gave it another blessing and watched it bound off into an Otherworld woodland as I continued on my own way. Encounters like these take milliseconds but leave a lasting impression.

The Other People are more conscious of the peculiarities of t ime than we tend to be. Therefore, they will sometimes leave you a gift intended for use later. When you see something out of place in your surroundings, perhaps a feather, a stone, or a shell on your doorstep or in your path, always accept it as a gift. Praise the gift verbally, such as:

Oh, what a lovely _____ *(stone, feather, etc.)!*
I know exactly where I can place (or how I can use) this!

—or something of that nature. When you have no clue what a gift is, try saying something about it that explains this but also accepts the gift with gratitude. One day I found a strange bit of something on my back porch that I could not identify, but it had a distinct gracefulness to it, so I said aloud, "I really appreciate this most unusual object! The energy is beautiful, but since I don't know what I will use this for at the moment, I will put this in my keepsake box and use it when the time is right." A year later, it was perfect for a charm bag. You can express yourself about a strange gift without identifying what it is, saying something like:

This is so very unusual and curious. I am intrigued,
but I have no idea what it is or how I will use
this, so I will place it in my special box for when
I become aware of what I am to do with this.

Be sure you are speaking the truth and from the heart because if your real impression is disdain, they will know and you will have severed an otherwise positive contact. If you think the object is weird or useless, reevaluate how to express gratitude.

Whether you recognize the unexpected item or not, it is a good plan to dedicate an attractive container for fairy gifts, one where you can store things until needed in Craft work. The one I have is wooden with a but-terfly wing design under a glass lid. I place fairy gifts in it until I need them for charms, spell candles, or other magical workings. At one time it was full of feathers, rocks, string, bits of colored gems, and shiny pieces of jewelry that had no reason to be at my doorstep, but over a period of just a couple of years I had found a purpose for most of the contents. Having your own special keepsake box will serve as a magical treasure chest from which you can withdraw an item when the inspiration or timing arrives.

Relating the Types of Other People to the Elementals

Different varieties of the Other People are closely associated with the elementals from Earth, Air, Fire, and Water, as they are seen working within or walking upon the earth, flying through the air, guarding sacred waters, and forging silver and gold. These correlations include, but are not limited to, the following:

- gnomes, tree devas, wood elves, or cobolds (or kobolds) for Earth
- sylphs, zephyrs, light elves, or cranes for Air
- phoenixes, will o' the wisps, blacksmith elves, or salamanders for Fire
- undines, nymphs, river elves, or selkies for Water

Trolls are usually considered rock people and thus relate to elemental Earth, but even if not viewed as rock related, they are still earth oriented. Cobolds are miners, so they relate to Earth, but they carry a fire with them to light their way, so they may also relate to Fire. Cranes are associated with Otherworld as guises for the Faerie beings who are wisdom keepers, thus relating to Air. Salamanders are considered the spirit that dwells within Fire.

The selection of representatives for the quarters during circle casting for ritual can be rather fluid, with the choices being up to the practitioner. I don't use dragons for fire, but I can cast a dragon circle with the different types and colors of dragons holding the quarters representing Earth at the north, Air at the east, Fire at the south, and Water at the west. There is also a more commonly used relation to the quarters with bull for Earth, eagle for Air, lion for Fire, and dolphin for Water.

Although you can identify the quarters with some Otherworld being, always be respectful of who you call upon. When working with the Other People, I may not use a mental image so as not to restrict our relationship, and instead I simply acknowledge whoever comes to hold that quarter.

I do not summon or banish but "call upon" and "farewell" with a blessing those who attend the rite and guard the circle. The Green Witchcraft courses I have taught vary from eight to thirteen weeks but are generally arranged to end on (or near) a sabbat, and I have had each class create their own personalized group ritual based on what I have demonstrated. I have been impressed by the students' attention to detail and their ability to organize and plan the ritual and carry it out to perfection. It is my hope that at least some of these people will go on to present the sabbats and esbats for their local community. The class students conduct a sabbat ritual with myself and sometimes with their family members in the circle, and usually the event ends with an initiation (in the sense of beginning a lifestyle) rite for those who choose.

. . . .

If you intend to summon and banish, be certain you have the methodology down pat.

At one such ritual, each quarter caller used their own method of invocation rather than a consistent one. There was one Craft-experienced person who summoned Fire as a lion with an invoking pentagram and did such a fine job that I saw the animal charge into position from another dimension and guard the south with an alert and ferocious expression. When it came time to open the circle, however, the caller hesitated while trying to remember the banishing pentagram for Fire. I saw the lion, fierce and ready to depart in a leap, change demeanor while the caller paused with athame raised in hand, poised to draw. The lion sat down, then stretched out on his belly, and, looking annoyed, drummed the floor with the digits of one paw. The caller finally remembered the procedure and completed the banishing, at which point the lion leisurely stood up, turned around, and slowly walked away, vanishing in a few steps. If you intend to summon and banish, be certain you have the methodology down pat. I feel that this type of calling implies the dominance of the caller over the elemental image, which may or may not accommodate, so while there was no harm done at this event, there is no telling how the lion might react to a future summons. Calling any elemental image at a quarter establishes a bond between yourself and a being from another world or dimension, and that relationship, especially in a Faerie-oriented ritual, is dependent upon good manners to be successful.

Out-of-Body Experiences

When working with energy, you are not actually focused so much on the objects of the magic as with the molecular structure that holds them together, wherein resides a part of Divine Spirit. Pantheism and animism acknowledge that Spirit is in everything, thus everything is alive. When science discovers a way to embrace or create a reasonable copy of a phenomenon, a definition is produced that makes it acceptable. Until a definition is created by science, people who undergo such things as an out-of-body experience (OBE) and near-death experience (NDE) are talked out of the reality of their spirit leaving their body by associating the event with a physical or mental condition—anything from a lack of oxygen to brain malfunction—so be circumspect with whom you discuss your experiences.

OBEs are not well received in society because people are generally terrified by the implication of spirits and souls being real. The spirit relates to the energetic part of you, while the soul relates to your self-awareness, or consciousness. If you harm someone in this life, can that person exact revenge in spirit while you are alive or attack you in spirit when you are also in spirit? The importance of offering forgiveness to those that harm you lies in bringing into balance the energy between you and that person. You ease the harmful person's energy field and increase your own spiritual light in the process. When people consider that their behavior in this life has a genuine effect on their actual existence after the body ceases to function, the basic concept of religious mandates to not kill or harm one another becomes real and immanent.

It is much easier to describe the evidence of OBEs and NDEs as psychological, physical, or mental aberrations than to call these real and have to deal with spirit, soul, and afterlife matters. The reality of life after death is inconvenient and frightening to a lot of people, especially those whose behavior in this dimensional existence has been harmful to others. Perhaps what drives some people to seek a way of prolonging the physical life is to postpone having to face the consequences of their actions in the afterlife.

The question of whether or not OBEs are actual phenomena is actively pursued by doctors and scientists in studies that mainly explain away the matter and translate a person's spirit and soul into merely a brain function or malfunction. Doing an internet search on "life after death" opens up many interesting discussions and scientific studies on the matter, as well as another subject that I will only touch upon here. Some have suggested that when a person dies, there is nothing, rather like when a person is put under anesthesia for surgery; others express a more open view that an afterlife is plausible, but there is no supporting scientific evidence and people are likely mistaken or misinterpreting what they experience. The United Kingdom's National Health Service has attributed NDEs to oxygen reaching the brain in patients receiving CPR.

Nevertheless, there are people who have been put under anesthesia who can recount all the goings-on during their surgery, having watched it from outside their bodies, usually high up by the ceiling of the operating room, for example. The fact that there is so much scientific research and investigation that tends to dismiss OBEs and NDEs shows the depth of the concern over the reality of spirit and soul. In 2019 another study described symptoms of NDEs and OBEs, including abnormal time perception, and concluded there was a relationship between these experiences and rapid eye movement (REM) indicating sleep intrusion into wakefulness, leading to hallucinations, the latter being a common symptom of NDEs and OBEs. Hallucinations with sound and sight, rapid thinking, and temporal distortion were identified as symptoms of sleep intrusion, but what about people who can deliberately leave their bodies or are wide awake and in the moment when time is distorted and visions occur, as with the automobile experiences mentioned in the first chapter? I feel that the only thing keeping people from initiating their own OBE is fear.

Over the years a few people have broached the subject of OBEs to me, usually with trepidation and hesitancy in their demeanor until they realize I am not going to call them crazy or debate with them about the legitimacy of what they experienced; then their eyes light up and their faces beam with joy and relief at being able to talk about their personal OBE. All of the psychological and scientific examination, attempts at re-creating an experimentally controlled OBE (in one case comparing an OBE with the moment before loss of consciousness when in a spinning centrifuge!), and data collection analysis may have a chilling effect on those who have experienced being out of their bodies and prevent them from talking about it to others. This in turn blocks others from gaining validation or confirmation that they, too, have actually left their bodies. People are pressured into silence by social explanations cultivated by research that deconstructs and reconstructs actual events with the result of diminishing the credibility of the person who has had an OBE.

The speed of departing and returning can be intentionally controlled in an OBE experience.

I used to have OBEs with a sudden departure and return, and one night while I was lying in bed thinking about a person who had told me about using OBEs as a way to go to concerts and explore distant lands, my spirit guide stood near my bedside and asked why I didn't like leaving my body. I explained that leaving and returning was very jolting to me. I was told it didn't have to be, that I could leave gently, and with that, my guide took me by my astral hand and I eased out of my body. I was surprised at how gentle it was and realized that the speed of departing and returning is something that can be intentionally controlled.

With an OBE, your spirit leaves your body and can travel anywhere at the speed of your thoughts. A person may have an OBE when their body is threatened and their spirit departs and hovers, waiting to see if the body survives and re-entering when it seems safe. Most people who confide in me about their OBE have found themselves at the ceiling in a corner of their bedroom looking down at their body in the bed below, and they are so alarmed by this that they return to their bodies in an unsettling snap. By initiating your own OBE, you can depart in a shot, as it were, or you can also depart smoothly, as I discovered. In leaving your body, you can see your spirit guide, Other People, and spirits, and travel where you desire simply by thinking about this.

Astral projection and astral travel are also OBEs, with astral projection indicating you stay close to your body or you go a distance away from your body yet remain in this world, while astral travel can be to any point in the universe or to another dimension or world. Again, you move to your desired destination at the speed of thought, so if you panic, your return trip will be abrupt, but if you remain calm and know that you are fine, you can go anywhere and meet up with animal spirits, guides and other spirits, or some of the Other People. Astral travel and projection might be considered more intentional than the usual surprise exit associated with OBEs, but I also see astral projection as a way of extending yourself into another area without leaving your body so you are basically in two places at the same time (as I did with the dead fox). Sometimes people see someone they know at one place only to discover that at the time the person was somewhere else. You can work on this type of astral projection by consciously visualizing where you would like to be, as with what I consider an active merging meditation wherein you deliberately blend your energy with a nearby object, such as a tree or a bird flying above you, to see things from their perspective.[4]

When you have an unexpected OBE, try not to panic. Instead, look at the situation surrounding your body, and if all feels well, then you could try moving around or asking for your spirit guide or other companion to visit with you. The more you connect with Otherworld energy, the more likely you are to start having this kind of event. If that is a problem for you, then you may not be ready to connect with the Other People. Approach with calmness and give yourself adjustment time so that you are more comfortable. Another side effect of an OBE is that you may start seeing spirits in passing or coming to you for assistance. Your spirit guide will "filter" visitors to keep you feeling secure.

Creating Your Own OBE

To experience a personally controlled OBE, I recommend a meditation beginning with your statement of intention: "I will move gently from my body without fear." Lie down comfortably on a sofa or bed as you choose. You could even place an astrophyllite (a stone for safe astral travel and return) in your power hand (the one you work with most or write with) or under the cushion or mattress to reassure yourself that you can travel and return to your body unharmed. Other useful stones include stellar beam calcite, which is a transparent clear, amber, or yellow version of opaque dogtooth calcite and has sharp points at one or both ends[5] and is an energetic stone for astral travel and gaining knowledge, especially when accompanied by moldavite and/or phenacite.

To depart on an OBE, close your eyes, take three cleansing deep breaths, using each breath to release tension, and relax. Clear your mind of miscellaneous chatter, relax, and visualize yourself as independent of your body, knowing that you can return at any time. Some people say

---

4   See chapter 9 of *Green Witchcraft II*.
5   As described and labeled on page 79 of *The Pocket Book of Stones* by Robert Simmons.

there is a slender silver cord that connects the spirit to the body during an OBE, so you may see this as well. Although I have not noticed this myself, that does not mean it isn't there, only that my attention has been elsewhere.

When you feel yourself relaxed to the point where you could almost fall asleep, try feeling yourself exiting or lifting out of your body. There is a peculiar sensation that goes along with the actual experience, so once you have successfully departed, you will recognize the feeling when getting close to having an OBE. As possible exit points, you could be pulling away gently through your mouth, nose, forehead, crown, torso, arm, leg, hand, or foot. It really doesn't matter where you depart from, but remember that you can move at the speed of thought, so try not to rush it. Traveling out of body can expend energy, so try not to go a long distance until you have successfully taken some short trips. You could move around the room, look down at your body from above, look at your spirit self in the mirror, or just check out the kitchen, but take the time to develop and hone your OBE skills.

We all have at least one spirit guide, and most people have several.

I was awakened one night at home by a loud thump coming from the next room. There had been a burglary nearby in the neighborhood, so I lay there wondering if this was an intruder but not wanting to get up and look. Instead, I eased out of my body. As I drifted past the dresser, I glanced at myself in the mirror, seeing my misty form floating along midway between floor and ceiling. At that moment I remembered that in spirit you can look like anything you desire, so I decided to look like a fierce and scary ghost. I immediately changed form and rushed into the next room ready to terrify any burglar lurking there. Instead, I saw that the cat had toppled over a large floor speaker and sat next to it looking perplexed. I resumed my normal shape with a giggle and quickly slipped back into my body. To me, this experience from many years ago disproves the previously mentioned 2019 hallucination or REM theory, for I was awake, and the next morning the speaker was still laid out on the floor where I had seen it during the previous night. Incidentally, I learned from this experience that changing your form will also drain you of some energy, so pay attention to your energy levels when doing that so you don't return with a jolt.

It may take some practice to get into that state where you are able to easily move outside your body, but once you have accomplished this, you will remember the sensation that predicates the exit, and this acts as a signal to you for future journeys. Prior to attempting an OBE, you may consider verbally asking your spirit guide to assist you in safely exiting your body. We all have at least one spirit guide, and most people have several. One of your guides will manifest to help. If you are uncertain about having an OBE, don't try to force it. Meditate on why you are afraid or why you should even bother. Not everyone is comfortable with that sort of travel, and although I have done so many times, I don't on any regular basis. There are other methods that can be used to travel or learn from the Akashic Records, but if you decide to utilize the OBE, remember to do so with the calm heart-set of love and the knowing mind-set of trust to enjoy a rewarding experience.

chapter

3

Connecting
with Faerie

Being open to communication, talking to plants, animals, and stones, requires a mind-set and heart-set that does not block this interaction. Just as when speaking with people you encounter during your daily life, talking with the Other People and the spirits within Nature is not scripted. You do not know what response you will receive to the things you say, and you should be open to understanding another's (an Other's) perspective. This is an opportunity for conversation, presenting your own views and hearing that of others, be they plant, stone, etc. Although magical practice often includes scripted or detailed formats, this is more to set the individual's mind in an altered state, one where the intonation of words stirs the energies. Ritual is for the practitioner, to aid in setting the atmosphere that takes a person out of the ordinary and into the magical. The same thing can be accomplished with simple conversation as long as your heart-set and mind-set are in balance and you speak from the heart. Simple words can be powerful when they come from the heart, spoken with love and sincerity as well as mental awareness.

Dropping the Barriers

By what mechanism is communication achieved, and how do you actually become open to interaction with the Other People and the spirits of Nature? To open the door, as it were, you can create a ritual for initiating communication with the Divine and the Other People by which you sweep aside the old way of life, with its skepticism and need for social and cultural conformity, and instead allow yourself to be reborn into a new way of life where you are confident and cognizant of the interconnection of all things through the energy of Spirit. You can follow a prescribed ritual or create your own rite in which you focus on changing from who you were to who you are to become, but you must be certain that contact with the Other People is what you desire, for it is your choice, and you alone are responsible for your actions.

To engage in a relationship and then decide to end it is the same with them as it would be in a human relationship, although it is difficult to predict how the Other People would react, how you might perceive their reaction would be and thus create it, or how you would be affected in the aftermath of cutting ties. When working with Faerie, returning to your previous state of doubt or cynicism where the Other People are concerned may have the same effect on a person as the loss of a loved one might have.

Because they have excellent manners, if you believe they will become angry and cause you to experience difficulties, that is what you will receive. A mind-set of Perfect Trust and a heart-set of Perfect Love are vitally important when working with the beings of Otherworld. When I messed up with the dragons, I absolutely knew they understood my personal disappointment with myself and I knew they forgave me, so our relationship began anew with better insight on my part. It is like an empathic connection where pride and arrogance have no more place than fear and blame, but these are replaced with understanding and energetic resonance.

Enter into this communication knowing that the God and the Goddess are not metaphors or archetypes; they are real, and they are in all dimensions and worlds throughout all universes. Rituals are tools to help us connect with the Divine, the Universal All. The elementals should also be included in the ritual at various stages since everything comes from the Divine and contains Divine Spirit (pantheism and animism). Since the Goddess and the God are present in all worlds and dimensions, when you make a commitment to the Divine, you become connected with all worlds and dimensions through them. It may take time for you to acclimate, so while some things may occur instantaneously, others may occur more gradually as you are ready to assimilate new insights and encounters. A ritual sincerely performed may open the way to frequent insight and assistance from the Divine and from the many inhabitants of the Otherworld. Each one of us is an individual with a unique life experience and perspective, so perhaps tweaking certain points in someone else's prepared ritual will work better for you. You have to trust your own intuition. Just because a ritual works for one person doesn't guarantee it will work for another, nor does it preclude using other methods or even experiencing a spontaneous connection.

The God and the Goddess are not metaphors or archetypes; they are real and in all dimensions and worlds.

Your interaction with the Goddess and the God, with the Other People, and with the creatures, plants, and objects of the natural world is a unique and personal event. What actually matters is your heart-set and mind-set—and yes, I keep pounding on this because it is so very important and vital to engagement. If you choose to create a ritual or make changes in an existing one, for whatever reason, ask the Divine to give you the inspiration to come up with suitable substitutions. Do this calmly when you have quiet time available or are about to go into a meditation. Ask your question, then put it out of your thoughts, gently brush aside any mental distractions, and relax. You can trust the Goddess and the God to answer in one form or another. They do not require rituals—those are for us—to help us focus and to alert our subconscious mind that something meaningful is happening.

Opening the Way Ritual

Spend some time contemplating your intention to open communication with the inhabitants of Otherworld through the power of the Goddess and the God. Think about what it is that worries you about this connection and what it is that you hope to find. Use this time to find answers to any questions you may have about removing the barrier between you and the Fair Folk, understanding that the Other People may include spirits, sentient creatures, plants, stones, and more beyond what you may imagine. Put aside your preconceived notions of what the inhabitants of Faerie should be like and instead be open to discovery. Address your fears and any concerns you may have, and if you decide not to continue, that may simply mean the current energy alignment is not appropriate for the ritual at this time or that you prefer or are better served at this time with your current lifestyle and worldview. Above all, trust the Goddess and the God.

Have all your needed supplies together at your altar and read through this ritual before you cast your circle. You can have the ritual written down on a paper if you choose. On the altar, have a pen and a piece of paper or parchment on which you first write "I, _____," leaving a blank space that you will later fill in with your new name. After the blank space, write your personally worded promise to open your mind to the voices of the Divine, the Ancient Ones, and the Other People, and to develop your magical skills. Place your besom close by the altar to sweep the space clear of negative and chaotic energies. Have the following on your altar:

- a white votive candle in a safe container
  (big enough to hold quickly melting wax)
- matches

- a needle or pin
- a small bowl of soil
- your tools of the Craft: athame to direct energy; bolline (a knife with straight or curved blade) to harvest herbs and inscribe tools; and wand to greet and farewell invited spirits, the elementals, and the Divine and also for channeling energy

If not using a wand, a staff may be used as a long wand. A stang (a staff with two or three branches at the top) may be used as a wand or an altar, stuck into the ground or held in a stand and decorated with vines and flowers, with incense and a candle on the ground at the base. The staff and stang are generally used in place of a wand and an altar, so these are individual preferences, not requirements. The wand can be used for much of the same purpose as the athame. The athame is generally used for channeling energy, but I also use mine for drawing magical symbols on candles prior to lighting. My bolline is used for cutting herbs and other utilitarian work.

The circle you cast acts as a boundary that sets your space apart from the ordinary world and makes the place within it sacred and secure for opening doorways to other dimensions. Circle casting can be as embellished or as simple as you like. A forefinger can work just as well as an athame. I normally cast the circle north, east, south, and west, but another option is beginning at the east, as with the sunrise. You must trust your own intuition as to where you begin. I place my altar at the north of the circle, but some people prefer the east. After the circle is cast, take your time for the rest of the ritual. Stand facing the altar and speak your intent to the Goddess and the God, asking for their blessings and for their opening the communication between them and you in the bonds of love.

Call upon elemental Air to receive your promise to open your mind to the voices of the Divine, the Ancient Ones, and the Other People, and to develop your magical skills.

Light the white votive candle and call upon elemental Fire to light your way into your new life, then set the candle on the floor or ground between you and the altar (give yourself room).

Lie down on your back at the foot of your altar and call upon elemental Earth to receive your body as someone who is departing from this life to enter into another.

With eyes closed, visualize sinking into the embrace of the earth, knowing that you are relinquishing your former life. See yourself as deep within the rich, dark soil, your body fading away into the earth. You may begin to feel an empty sensation or you may even cry as you visualize releasing your prior kind of life, feeling your spirit moving into the Land of Shadows.

Think of elemental Water and see in your mind the sacred waters of the earth—the seas, natural springs, and waterfalls—and feel these waters wash over you, cleansing and refreshing your spirit. Feel yourself floating with ease in the blessed waters of life.

Think of yourself as part of the Divine Spirit and carefully move into a fetal position so you are now facing the candle in preparation for your rebirth. Open your eyes and look at the candle, seeing the flame as the God of Light who, like the sun, travels a yearly path through the cycles of the earth, through the equinoxes and solstices, leading the way for us to understand that life is an eternal cycle. See yourself moving from the womb of the earth to be birthed through the Goddess into a new life in the Light of the God. Sit up, stand when you're ready, and take the candle with you and set it in the center of the altar.

Close your eyes and call upon the Goddess and the God to name you:

> *As parents name their children, so do I,*
> *as your child, seek your naming of me.*
> *Lady and Lord, tell me: What is my name?*

The name you receive is a secret and a sacred trust between you and them, so do not share that name with anyone. Acknowledge their gift of a new name, and seal your connection by writing your secret name in the blank space of the paper on which you previously wrote your promise. Kiss the paper and burn it in the votive flame. This paper is the ONLY time you will write out your secret name. Pull out a couple of your hairs and burn these in the flame. Sterilize the tip of the needle or pin in the flame, prick the tip of the little finger of your left hand, and squeeze out a few drops of blood onto the soil in the bowl, which is to be emptied on the ground later. In modern times we know that hair and blood contain the DNA that identifies a person, but these are symbols used since ancient times to represent the earth and water elements of a person, while the promise and flame it is consumed within represent the air and fire elements. You are making a commitment and sealing it with the essences that represent you.

The Secret Name

From now on, the secret name is quietly used only in private communication between you and the Lady and the Lord, while your Craft name is one that you have selected for public or group use in ritual and magical practice as desired. You may ask the Goddess and the God by which names you may address them. You might get names, or see them, or you might learn the names as you follow your path. You must protect your secret name by never writing it down or engraving it onto anything. You never know when someone might stumble on it, and there is no point in taking chances. In ancient tradition, if another person knows this name, it can give that person power over you. This is not a test for trusting someone, nor is it something to take lightly. You must NEVER reveal your secret name to ANYONE, including the Other People, for the name DEFINES you.

The secret name echoes the ancient tradition that forbids asking the Fair Folk their names. This is seen vividly in the familiar Grimm Brother's fairy tale of Rumpelstiltskin, the core of which is said to date back at least five thousand years. The Other People have secret names, but as they are unable to lie, asking them to give you their names is tantamount to demanding to be given power over them, which is both unwise and ill-mannered. Instead of receiving an answer, the questioner could be abandoned, left to flounder aimlessly and lost in a less than friendly Otherworld.

When seeking a way to identify or talk to one of the Other People, ask "How may I address you?" or "By what name may I address you?" and you will receive what amounts to a Craft name in Otherworld. Often the Fairy name describes an attribute, talent, object, animal, or plant, such as Harper, Songstress, Shield, Blade, Stone, Moonglow, Ivy, and so on. But as to the names that define them, that is a secret between each one and the Divine in their aspects of Goddess and God of Faerie, be these Lady and Lord of Shadows, Lady of Nature and Lord of the Greenwood, Green Lady and Green Man, Queen of the Sea and King of the Mountain, Lady of the Meadow and Lord of the Wildwood, or even familiar Fairy names like Queen Titania and King Oberon.

I cannot guarantee what your own experience will be like; for me, the Goddess and the God appeared when I asked them to name me, and she did. I could not grasp it, so I asked, "Can you spell that for me?" and she did. I had reached emotional overload, however, and I made a silly remark that resulted in what sounded and felt like the slam of a door, and I was suddenly alone at my altar, with the atmosphere abruptly changed to normalcy. I took a few moments to calm down, then I gave a heartfelt apology and continued with the ritual from the point of interruption, writing the name on the paper and burning it, followed by a few strands of my hair plucked from my head.

The instant a couple drops of my blood touched the soil in the bowl, a large, serene, dark lake appeared in front of me, and opposite was a narrow shore with a dark, leafy forest behind it. In front of the woodland I saw (as I faced it) two straight trees with leafless branches: a dark one on the left side and a white one on the right side. In front of the dark tree stood the white-gowned, luminous Goddess, while in front of the white tree stood the bare-chested, shadowy God. I heard him say, "Never be afraid of making mistakes because we love you." In that moment I felt a great sense of relief and joy, and all I desired was to be with them. That feeling sent me swiftly flying across the lake and into the welcoming, strong arms of the God. I was very reluctant to leave that embrace, with his arms around me and my head resting against his broad chest, but I absolutely knew that I could not stay. He gently released me, and I asked the Goddess (who I felt I had offended) if she would let me embrace her. She gave me a kind, gentle hug, and I felt a mystical sensation of mossy coolness and lunar stillness. I shot back across the lake and the scene vanished. I do not recall this experience as being out of body, for all of my senses were totally engaged and this remains a singular event.

The Goddess and the God continue to come to me, individually or together. When I need help or advice, I may receive counsel from any number of sources, be they the elementals, Other People, spirits, entities, or even the Goddess or the God (or both) appearing in aspects appropriate for the matter at hand and always generous with wisdom and gentle guidance. People have told me about their own very personal encounters with the Divine, and for some it came through ritual or meditation or spontaneously, so there are different paths to the same destination. For psychologists and scientific researchers, an ecstatic spiritual experience is an anomaly of the mind, but I feel the mind might present a symptom of actual events and that researchers incorrectly interpret the symptom as the event itself. Like OBEs, unless someone has done this, hearing about it may seem improbable or delusional, which is why I suggest you "be careful who you trust" with this kind of information.

Pacing the Realm

I tend to be more intuitive oriented in my magical workings, so I don't keep all of the material in my grimoire at the forefront of my thoughts. However, I do like to check back later for validation that the correlations I made intuitively were in alignment when creating crafts, charms, or spells. When someone asked me how to clear negativity from a large new property without offending the land spirits and Fairy Folk, I instantly

81

thought of parsley, rue, and rosemary, and I saw that the herbs needed to be scattered across the property. To me, this felt like a direct message from the Other People, so I just went with it. I told the person to pace the realm and sprinkle the herbs across the land, that this was the information I received, but let me look it up to be sure, and in my herbal listing I saw that this was definitely the perfect combination: parsley for purification and protection, rue to consecrate and ward negativity, and rosemary for blessing and connecting with the elves. I explained that pacing the realm is a fairy custom, which may relate to the legends of trooping fairies and the fairies moving from one location to another twice a year, along with the warning for humans to stay out of their way and off their known roads (mainly the ley lines of earth energy).

• • • • • • •

Pace your realm to let the nature spirits recognize your energy and kinship.

The Fair Folk pace the realm in order to re-energize the boundaries between their world and this world, or to reinforce possession of their particular lands within Otherworld. Typically, the Other People will walk, ride, or fly along the borders of their territory. In the Middle Ages, and to some extent in modern times, processions were carried out by royalty to reinforce their authority over their realm and let the populace know that their rulers were actively engaged with the land and its inhabitants. These processions usually entailed the ruler travelling with a large retinue of court nobles and soldiers, dropping in on the local lords to be royally lodged, fed, and entertained at great expense to the lesser nobility. This kept the nobles in line and possibly depleted their funds to keep their local armies at a minimum and thus not a threat to the power of the ruler. I feel that since trooping fairies were long established in folklore, human rulers took up the example for their own ends. King Henry VIII and his daughter, Queen Elizabeth, were famous for their processions in England.

We can also pace our own realms, however large or small, and let the nature spirits recognize our energy and that we belong there in kinship with them. Walking along the border of your property, or riding around it if large, creates an energy wall that the Other People may pass through with ease and also alerts the land spirits to know who you are. When in a compatible relationship with Nature, land, and Otherworld, your property is protected energetically against unwanted intruders. You should do this activity at least annually, and you can augment the pacing with yard work, sprinkling herbs along the path, planting desired crystals in the four corners of the property, and other such energetic magics.

When you pace the realm, you are putting into the land (or floor for condo owners) an energy footprint that marks the territory as yours and sets your property aside as sacred space, rather like casting a circle. For people who rent, the land or property belongs to someone else, but you can still place crystals, stones, and herb packets in the corners of the rooms or windowsills to act as wards (protective energy shields) as you walk around your dwelling or rental property. Options include smoky quartz for crystals, red jasper for stones, and rosemary or fennel for herbs, to name but a few.

When placing herbs or crystals around your territory, be sure these are appropriate to encourage friendly visits from the Other People. Besides walking around your property, you can also grow thorny plants and vines such as briar, nettles, or thistles in key locations as your intuition directs to attract the Fair Folk and offer protection as well. Trefoil or shamrocks grown in a pot or in the yard offer protection while also attracting fairies. At Lughnassadh (August 1, also called Lammas) a sheaf of consecrated wheat can be placed were desired (usually hung in the home) for good fortune, but each year the old sheaf needs to be scattered in the property and replaced by a new one.

Although you can plant herbs, when pacing the realm you should scatter the dried herbs as you go around the border of your property. Herbs from the spice rack are perfectly fine for this, as are crushed shells from certain nuts, cut-up bark or roots, and seeds. Some suggestions to choose from, singularly or in combination (3, 7, or 9, generally), include:

- alder leaves (invokes fairies)
- anise (consecrates and invokes spirit aid)
- apple blossoms/seeds/slices (attracts protective unicorns)
- basil (repels negativity)
- clover leaves or flowers (consecration and Otherworld connection)
- elderflowers or berries (attracts fairies, blessings, and enhances magical power)
- elm leaves (attracts elves)
- fennel (deflects negativity)
- ginger (enhances power of other herbs)
- hawthorn berries or hazelnuts/shells (attracts fairies, enhances witchery)
- lavender (cleansing, inviting to elves)
- marigold flowers (fairy protection, enhances psychic ability)
- mint leaves (offering to helpful spirits)
- mugwort (consecration, protection, strength)
- parsley (purification, protection)
- rosehips (love, psychic power)
- rosemary (protection, blessing, purification, attracts elves)
- rowan leaves/berries (invokes spirit help, home protection)
- rue leaves (blessing, consecration, wards negativity)
- sage leaves (purification, aid of power animal guides)
- sandalwood (spirit offering, wards negativity)
- Solomon's seal/dropberry (elemental offering, protection)

- sunflower petals/seeds (good prospects, consecration, help from elves, purifying)
- vervain (purification, offering, wards psychic attack)
- yarrow flowers/leaves/roots (defense, protection, ward negativity)

While it is common to use crystals and stones as corner boundary markers, you can also drop them on the ground or push them into the soil as you pace. If your property has a lot of cement area, setting the stone in a safe place, such as in a flower pot or on a table, is an option. The size of the crystal or stone is a matter of personal preference and convenience. The energy works whether the stone is large or small. Some suggestions for stones that not only protect the property but are also Other Folk-friendly include smoky quartz (Faerie connection, draw positive energy), black tourmaline (protection against psychic attack), and red jasper (protection and strength), which is fine to place on a windowsill. Sunlight will fade amethyst, citrine, and smoky quartz, and direct sunlight could cause some stones to fragment, so, to me, red jasper is perfect. Cleansing with spring water requires knowing the properties of the stones, for some, such as covellite and selenite, will dissolve in water.

It is common to use crystals and stones as corner boundary markers, and you can also push them into the soil.

While anything of iron is considered a ward against fairies, this may be more of a human tradition born from the advent of the Iron Age replacing the Bronze Age, often with devasting warfare where the superior iron weapons of invaders forced the local inhabitants into submission. Iron production and weapon making, particularly that of swords, was historically a highly guarded secret, and as such caused iron to be perceived as a magical metal, possibly associated with meteor iron and thus from the stars and the gods. Blacksmiths were held in awe for their ability to turn stone into tools and weapons, inspiring such smith deities as Roman Vulcan, Greek Hephaestus, Norse Volund, Germanic Wieland, and the Faerie blacksmith Wayland Smith, an elf lord of the Icelandic sagas. With this latter inclusion, it appears that iron may not actually have any ill effect on the Other People as superstition has supposed (using iron to ward them off); however, they are traditionally known to prefer the beauty and shine of silver and gold.

Another way to let the Fair Folk know you are open to their visitations is to grow rosemary by your door or place it there as a potted plant. Rosemary grows into a large shrub if planted but can be carefully trimmed with permission. Ask the plant if you can trim it and which sprigs you may cut, then prune where you feel the plant is directing you. Rinse the cuttings off, tie them together, and hang the sprigs upside down to dry in a cool place out of direct sunlight. Once dried, you can easily strip the leaves off and store them in a jar for use in magical cooking, oils, spells, and charms. Lavender flowers attract the Fair Folk with a clean, fresh fragrance they enjoy. Herbs such as marjoram, thyme, basil, and parsley are also favored. Indeed, working in a garden, be it with herbs, flowers, or vegetables, will draw them to you, so seek their blessings and those of the nature spirits to have your garden thrive.

Creating Fairy Sacred Space

It is easy to create an outdoor shrine for the fairies when you have your own yard. If yard space is not available, you can create a place in your dwelling where you honor the Fair Folk and nature spirits. For over thirty-five years I have used a piece of driftwood as a fairy altar in the yard. It has a flat portion that on one end sweeps up into a bare forked branch. I set an offering bowl on the flat part and hang decorations from the overhanging forked branch—usually crystal beads on a silver strand. The driftwood altar has traveled across the country with me and has enhanced many a yard as I moved from one location to another. It is finally starting to show its age as the branch has dipped and the girth has shrunk, yet it still serves as a place for shiny gifts. Now there is a stone garden fairy statue in front of it, and offerings are placed by her. I expect the altar will dissolve into the land in another year or two, and that will further enhance the energies of the property.

Indoors you can have a special place or shrine to honor the Other People. The traditional animist religion of Shinto in Japan honors the nature spirits, and there are shrines around the forests and rivers dedicated to the protector animals of the area. These little alcoves may contain images of foxes or other creatures, or even of Fairy Folk, although not called that. These days it is easy to find beautiful fairy figurines or stone images for an indoor shrine or special place in the home or yard. Placing some of the above-listed stones with the figurines, lighting a candle, or placing a bowl of water or milk in front of the figurine at the full and dark moons will keep the connecting energy flowing.

Those unexpected objects that you encounter near your door or on your path are fairy gifts.

Additionally, staurolite, a rare natural brown cross called fairy cross or fairy tears, is a good stone to add to the shrine, as is menalite, called both a fairy stone and a goddess stone and relating to the Earth Mother and transitions (be these dimensional or life). Menalite is unusual as it has a soft covering of tiny filaments that will acquire a smooth texture from the oils of your hand if you pet it. This stone is not very common and is creamy, white, or grayish in color, looking rather like connected blobs that are suggestive of a form, such as a manatee, a turtle, or a goddess, rather like seeing images in the clouds. The stone is so inviting that petting is a natural response, so don't be upset if the filaments become smoothed down—it could actually be a way to create a connection between yourself and the fairy stone. With stones in general, I suggest not letting other people handle yours since they may impart their own energies and thus require you to cleanse the stone with the smoke of sage smudge or other preferred method. This also applies to ritual jewelry and your personal tools of the Craft.

Fairy gifts, those unexpected objects that you encounter near your door or on your path, may be placed on the shrine, then stored for use in ritual or magic work. Pictures and images of the Fair Folk placed there or around the dwelling lets them know you are Otherworld friendly. You may discover you are drawn to a number of fantasy books relating to fairies, but be careful not to get caught up in someone else's agenda or vision of what is or is not typical of the Other People.

By showing respect for the wild, you draw the attention and blessings of the Other People.

Having a wild place in your yard is another good way to connect with the Other People. While they do appreciate and reward tidiness in a yard, there is also a need to balance the weeded and manicured with a portion that is overgrown, offering a hiding place for birds, rabbits, and other small creatures. By showing respect for the wild in wildlife, you draw the attention and blessings of the Other People. Knowing that nature spirits thrive in shrubs, trees, and wild grasses lets them know that they are included in your connection with Nature.

The wild space I kept at one house became the nursery for the ducks from the local pond. There were duck nests tucked away under the wild-growing ginger plants, trees, bushes, and vines, and every year the mommy ducks taught their babies to swim in the overgrown little decorator yard pond. Once a duckling was unable to hop back out of the pond, so adding a piece of board at the side became a ramp for ducklings. To me, the fact that wild ducks were comfortable in the yard was symbolic of Faerie blessings and good fortune. Cranes showed up as well, and they are symbolic of peace, happiness, and wisdom, but they are also a traditional guise for the Fair Folk. When you find that particular animals, birds, or insects like your territory, it is good to investigate the energies associated with them.

In your own home, you can create a wild space by not being overly aggressive to the insects that are helpful. I am not a particular fan of spiders, but I do know they eat bugs, so I allow what I call "corner spiders" to dwell in some of the rooms. When I encounter a useful spider (not poisonous ones) indoors, I say it is welcome but needs to build its web in a particular corner. I coax it into a paper cup and drop it off where desired, and every spider I have done this with has built its web and remained in its designated location. From time to time I might even greet the spider in its corner and ask how it's doing or compliment it on doing a good job.

One evening I saw a small black fuzzy spider on the high ceiling of my bedroom and I simply knew it was one of the corner spiders I had set in place awhile back. Without any explanation, I also knew that it would work its way across the large room and over the bed, and I said aloud, "You're going to stay up there all night to die and fall on my face while I'm asleep." The spider's message was sweet: "I did my work for you, and I have come to say goodbye." Sure enough, I was later awakened when it died and fell from the ceiling, landing on my face, but I was not alarmed. I set the little corpse outside in the garden. Sometimes you can find a gentle rapport in unexpected places.

Vortices and Ley Lines

If your area has either an energy vortex (a swirling energy like water in a whirlpool) or a ley line (a straight path of energy) running through it, coming into contact with these can make time feel faster or slower but can also have positive or negative effects on people, such as causing people to feel unsteady on their feet or mentally confused, as with losing a train of thought or drawing a blank. A vortex can be a natural phenomenon or one that someone creates and is considered good for enhancing meditation or self-understanding; however, it can also be a portal for spirits or a crossing point from one dimension into another. If you have such a spot in your property, you might be able to encounter

Otherworldly beings and spirits in this place, and it could be a good site for a shrine or one of the stones previously mentioned.

Creating a vortex can have unsettling potential if you fail to close it or guard it with protective stones if leaving it open. As long as you have protections in place or protectors guarding it, the vortex may be useful for meditation, astral travel, lucid dreaming, and contacting spirits. When finished with the purpose of the vortex, be sure to close it, even if only temporarily should you desire to keep the portal functional, just so the next person who enters the area is not caught off-balance. Losing your balance or your train of thought in an area is a typical reaction by the unawares to an open vortex.

To create a vortex, begin by releasing stress and grounding that energy. Decide what you want the vortex to accomplish and for what purpose you are creating it, such as spirit communication, dimensional or astral travel, deep meditation, protection, etc. Set a crystal or stone that feels appropriate at the center, using the stone's energy correlation to match your intent (see list in next section). You can smudge the location clockwise (to draw in; for travel or protection, for example) or counter-clockwise (to draw out; negativity or unwelcomed lingering influences from prior habitation, for example) when you open the vortex, and in the reverse direction when you close it. Smudging clockwise around the center stone, say:

> *This space is cleansed so that earth energies of (protection, travel, etc.) may be activated to aid me in my work.*

Visualize energy swirling in the direction you smudge, and when you feel there is sufficient energy, you can proceed with the purpose for which you created the vortex.

Placing two mirrors facing each other can also open a vortex and create a way for any passing entity to slip into the area, rather like leaving the front door to your dwelling wide open. Department stores can still be found that have dressing rooms where a customer can stand in front of three mirrors for simultaneous view of front and both sides. By looking in the mirrors at an angle, you can see yourself repeated into the distance. If you leave mirrors facing each other in your home or other area, they will reflect each other into the distance, creating an unguarded portal. If passing dimensional visitors have not departed, such portals could account for suggestions of hauntings or paranormal activity in an area even after the mirrors are removed.

To close a portal, first smudge the area with white sage or a combination of the sage and dragon's blood or sage and lavender leaves, and say:

> *This space is cleared so that no energies*
> *that may be harmful to me or to others*
> *may pass through into this place.*

Once smudged, if the vortex came from facing mirrors, you can now remove one mirror and relocate it. The sage can next be passed around the vortex in the opposite direction that the energy seems to be spinning. You may use a pendulum to see in which direction it spins, then sage in the opposite direction as you visualize the energy slowing down and retreating into the earth (or ground under a building), then dissipating into the land to be reused by Nature. Check again with the pendulum, which should now remain still.

A ley line is considered to be a natural straight line of energy that connects geographic points, and while there is much debate as to whether or not such lines are coincidental or meaningful, the tradition of the Fairy Road hearkens to this being an ancient understanding that received the more modern term in the early 1920s. Considered to be natural earth energy streams, the locations where these lines intersect can be centers of power capable of enhancing psychic experience and creating dimensional portals. If this intersection is in your home or property, keep mirrors out of it to ensure the energy is not reflected into your space. Next, you can create a "junction box" for the ley lines to pass through without disturbing your area. Visualize the lines as entering their individual tunnels or conduits, rather like what an electrician might run a cable through in a building. Visualize the energy lines intersecting with their separate conduits so one goes over the other, rather like an overpass on a highway, with the other line passing underneath where the lines cross each other. By visualizing the energy lines as encased but freely flowing in their conduits only on your property or in your space, you minimize the energy disruption. If you plan to use the intersection as a dimensional portal or for psychic connections, leave it as you encountered it. If it becomes bothersome, utilize the conduits.

When creating the conduit, I like to use my hands to define the conduits since the palms of the hands are great for conducting energy, and the tube is basically an energy encasement. Stand next to the ley line at the place you desire to begin the conduit, holding your hands about two feet apart with palms facing each other, then slowly bring your hands closer together, visualizing a tubular energy field encircling the ley line. Keep repeating the process as you walk along the ley line to where you desire to end the conduit. Do the same for the crossing ley line and move it over or under the previously created conduit.

I have shown people how to create energy fields with a simple exercise. Use your hands to gather energy into a large ball that you can then compact into a smaller size, such as like a baseball, fashioning it as you would making a snowball or a doughball. With the energy ball contained between your hands, focus into it something you would like to manifest, then release the ball upward with a quick underhand toss to the Universe.

Because the Other People are basically in a different or parallel dimension, they can pass in a straight line from one point to another in this dimension without hinderance, going through buildings, fences, and so on. The warning of not building on a known Fairy Track or Road is meant to prevent the unpleasant side-effects manifested in this world as a result of such Otherworldly travels. Materially, a Fairy Road may destabilize the land on which a structure might be built, even to the point of causing it to collapse. Within a house, the inhabitants could experience nightmares, misfortune, debilitating illness, or "hauntings." Traditional prohibitions against building or lingering in areas where Otherworld travelers are known to pass also relates to the energy of the ley lines and is meant to protect people from those energies that can disrupt the human nervous system and cellular structure. While a structure built on such a site can crumble, the human body may suffer a lowering vitality or degradation of the immune or nervous systems, or issues with the very cells of the body. The effects can be minimized out of doors by burying a large amethyst or an amethyst cluster close to a ley line or in the area where the ley lines intersect. If the ley line intersection is indoors, you can place the amethyst in that area, avoiding exposure to direct sunlight. The stone will help elevate the energy so it passes at a higher level rather than the one where you are located.

Fairy Stones and Charm Bags

For Otherworld workings, magic, and ritual, you can choose to augment your work with the aid of one or two stones appropriate to your endeavor carried in hand or placed nearby.

Merlinite, a dendritic white agate with black psilomelane in it, enhances psychic power and communication with Nature spirits and entities.

Other useful stones include:

- astrophyllite (protection and guidance in astral travel, OBE, and dream travel)

- fluorite (Faerie realms, grounding)

- iolite (psychic power, astral travel)

- kyanite (altered states, manifestation)

- moldavite (a meteorite glass for dimensional travel)

- moonstone (psychic ability)

- black obsidian (benevolent healing, Otherworld/ Shadowland)

- rainbow obsidian (journeying)

- opal (astral travel, psychic power)

- peridot (occult power, inner vision)
- petalite (astral/dimensional travel)
- golden quartz (cleansing, spirit communication)
- rose quartz (peace, companionship)
- stellar beam calcite (interdimensional travel/Akashic Records)
- tanzanite (contact spirits and Otherworld beings)
- tiger eye (harmony)
- topaz (psychic insight)
- pink tourmaline (friendship)

Another object that is useful for Faerie work is the holey stone. This is a stone that has a naturally formed hole going clear through it. The tradition is that it is a river rock, but sea rock also works well. There is an old custom for Beltane (May 1) and Litha (Midsummer Eve/summer solstice) wherein you can stand beneath an elder tree, carefully dab a bit of rosemary water above or below your eye (don't get it into your eye), and look through the hole to see the fairies. Some customs specify other trees, such as rowan, ash, or hazelnut. Since the Fair Folk are everywhere, the tree may be one that you are drawn to by your intuition. Learn to trust your intuition. The stone can be used for protection from negative energies but also to look between the worlds and gain the aid of the Other People in times of need.

When it comes to ritual, Beltane and Litha are good times for realigning with the Fair Folk through ceremony and focus. You could even have special tools that are used only for Faerie rituals and magics, such as an obsidian, jasper, jet, or crystal-bladed athame, a wood wand of elderwood (but not cut from a tree unless permission is granted), hazel, hawthorn, elm, willow, birch, or ash (with or without crystal/gemstone embellishments), a chalice of silver, pottery, or wood, and so on, relying more on objects made of copper, silver, gold, pottery, or natural substances such as pods, shells, and gourds. For the metals, you could call upon Wayland Smith for aid in acquiring the tool that is right for you. You could add seeds to your circle casting and focus on the circle as a fairy ring. One year I dropped small wooden mushrooms along the ground as I cast the faery ring, and many of the energized tokens were joyfully taken home by attendees.

I also like to make Faerie charm bags for people to take home for their personal altars, to place in the home, or to hang from a tree in their yard. The charm bag may be energized during the Beltane or Litha rituals, or during the waxing to full moon to encourage pleasant interaction with the Fair Folk. A charm bag may be made from a square of lavender or floral-patterned cloth (for sensitivity to Otherworld) and tied with a pale green ribbon (for Nature and fairy magics). Begin by laying out a 5- to 6-inch square of cloth. Lay on the cloth a small moonstone or purple stone such as fluorite, agate, or amethyst, and say:

> *This stone represents the connection and*
> *magic between the Other People and me.*

Add to the cloth a pinch of each of the following seven herbs, saying while dropping the herb:

> *Star anise for the Star of Otherworld, rosemary*
> *for attracting the Fair Ones, lavender for*
> *purification, fennel for the God, elderflower for*
> *the Goddess, mugwort for psychic enhancement,*
> *and rue for consecration and blessing.*

As you gather the ends of the cloth together and tie with ribbon or yarn, say:

> *With the energies of these herbs, may there be*
> *balance and joy between the Fair Folk and me.*

Place your hands, palms down, over the charm bag:

> *This charm is consecrated through the Goddess and the God,*
> *through the elementals Earth, Air, Fire, and Water, that*
> *there be communication between the Folk of Otherworld*
> *and me. With blessings given and received, so mote it be.*

Offerings and Gifts

In Celtic lands, people prayed to the elves for protection, for healing, and for the well-being of the herds and the home. The mounds were a place for making offerings to the elves, be it the sacrifice of a bull with the blood sprinkled around, a gift of milk and honey, or one of milk and bread. In Scandinavia, the sacrifice to the elves was part of a petition for help, protection, and fertility called an *álfablót*, with the typical offering to the elf god Freyr being a boar, bull, or ox, and for the Dísir (female deities, land spirits, and maternal ancestors), at a *disablót*, a pig, but also honey, sweets, and amber were appropriate as associated with the goddess Freya (Freyr's sister). Eating ham has remained a traditional food at Yule or Ostara, both critical periods when the forces of Nature and fertility needed to be honored and encouraged. The elven rituals of Scandinavia were mainly private in Pagan times, held by families in their homes, rather like holidays today for Christmas (Yule) and Easter (Ostara), when families come together to have a special meal, but there were also public gatherings and sacrifices at the temple in Uppsala, Sweden. Today, offerings to the Other People are personalized by the solitary practitioners of the Craft or by the customs of various covens (small groups of practitioners who meet for ritual and work magic together).

Offerings can be a way of extending an invitation to the Other People to visit or dwell nearby.

Offerings can be a way of extending an invitation to the Other People to visit or dwell nearby. You could be seeking to join in their celebrations or ask for their aid in your Craft work or their blessing in your home and life. You could use the offering as an expression of kinship and to show appreciation for their being kindly disposed toward you and your family. Oatmeal, milk, wheat, herbs, flowers, or wine are still considered appropriate offerings to the Other People, given to honor their friendship or solicit their aid. Setting out of doors a bowl of milk in a particular place on the night of the full moon is a custom of long standing. In the morning, finding that overnight a fairy ring (circle of mushrooms) has sprung up around the bowl is seen as evidence that the Fair Folk danced in the yard. We normally would set out a bowl of milk on nights of the full moon, however I have varied the offerings as my intuition directs and the weather warrants. In chilly weather I have left a small bowl of Irish Mist whiskey or wine for the Other People, while other times, in a hot and humid season, I have left outside a bowl of well water. Other offerings include liqueur, beer, herbs, cookies, and biscuits.

We have a custom of not being concerned with saving every bit of food and drink, but sharing with the spirits, with Nature, and with the Other People. When indoors, we also say that what food falls to the floor is for the Other People or a libation to the house fairies. Keeping a bowl of water for the deities along with a special dish with a cookie, biscuit, or even a sweet reinforces our connection and communion. At Yule I offer a bit of my homemade fruitcake and wassail, for example, while at Imbolc milk and buttered bread are left on the hearth. Trust your own intuition as to what offering is best for the occasion. Any beverage or food set out for the deities, the Other People, spirits, or nature entities are not to be consumed by people, for the essence has been consumed, leaving only a "husk" behind to be disposed of the next day. Offerings are made to acknowledge the presence of the Other People and the benefits they bestow through their benevolence and helpfulness. Pouring a libation on the ground is another type of offering that honors the spirits and Other People around us.

The giving of gifts is a recognition of favorable energy alignments. Tokens of appreciation for the Other People may include silvery, shiny, glittery objects and sparkly gemstones. A silver dime or a bit of quartz crystal make good gifts for outdoor shrines. This is not a one-way communication, for fairy objects will often come to people who are open to the Other People and receptive to their visits. These can be as simple as a feather or pretty stone appearing at the front or back door of the home or as refined as a small seed pod bowl, a stone cup, or even a ring. By leaving a gift for the fairies, you may be inviting them to dwell nearby, asking for their aid in your Craft work, seeking their blessing, sending an expression of appreciation for previous help, or simply acknowledging the kinship of all beings.

chapter

4

Working with the Other People

W hen addressing the Fair Folk, I feel that it is best to keep the Old Ways unencumbered by mainstream infusions. It is very disconcerting to find references to fairies that are created out of a mainstream religion association cobbled onto the Other People, especially since most of these reduce the energetic relationship with fairies into terms intended to inspire fear and trepidation and thus sever the connection. These negative associations, such as the Seelie Court, Unseelie Court, and Red Caps discussed earlier, are meant to intimidate and discourage people from making connections or communicating with the Other People or spirits. People who are psychic may be called possessed, people who see or talk to spirits may be told they have demonic attachments, and on it goes, with the outcome of instilling fear and bringing the individual back into social/cultural/religious conformity. Do not presume because you have a bad experience that something external is out to get you. Perhaps you are attracting negative energies because you walk in fearfulness, or this may have been something you agreed to between lives for karmic reasons or to raise your spiritual light through overcoming this obstacle.

Encountering the Other People

I feel it is better to not have preconceived ideas of what the Other People are like, for some may come across as grotesque looking (in the style of Rembrandt's sketches of people called Grotesques) but are quite friendly and helpful. If you judge people by their appearances and follow a social construct of good-looking means nice and strange-looking means bad, you may need to reconsider any attempt at entering Otherworld. The artwork of Arthur Rackham, depicting different types of fairies with long fingers, narrow or broad faces, thin or plump bodies, pointed ears or noses, and broad smiles or closed mouths, doing ordinary things— looking engaged in their work, kindly disposed, bored with humans, annoyed, or joyful in unfettered revelry—may help you to better understand the unusual appearances that might be adopted by the Fair Folk. This could even be a test to see if you are biased or willing to engage with people who look different before letting you into their circle. When I saw the hairy grogan in my house, I sensed at once that he was a helpful and kindly Fair One, although he was not inclined to be seen and disappeared quickly. Like us, each one of the Other People has a distinct personality.

It is also more likely that when you first encounter one of the Other People, you might not recognize the nature of the person until later. Just as I stated earlier that you don't need to learn foreign or archaic languages to talk to aspects of the deities or to the Other People, you should not expect them to dress in what was high fashion in the fifteenth century of the current era. The Other People are not fixed in a time period but change and adapt through the centuries, and given their ability to change appearance, you can be sure they change fashion styles. Remember, too, my earlier remark about the three elderly men who appeared out of nowhere over a period of three years to give me the same message three times. While each one looked like an ordinary person, there was an unusual energy to them, or presence, that made me feel they were not human, and I greeted them with respect and received their messages with gratitude.

When looking at old fairy tales, one that raises an eyebrow for me includes an encounter with a "little gray man" by a young man in the forest seeking the waters of life to save his dying father. The gray man helps him achieve his goal, and today this description matches what we might call a gray alien. Fairy-tale descriptions of the Other People vary, but the suggestion that even attractive human-looking Fair Folk will have some deformity, such as cloven feet or a shallow back, are more likely intended as intimidation to keep people from actively engaging in communication with the Other People. Try not to have preconceived ideas of the People you will encounter, but instead allow them to manifest as they choose and accept that with love and trust. There is an Arthurian tale of a knight forced to wed a hag, but because he is an honorable man, he treats her with dignity and respect.

Try not to have preconceived ideas of the People you will encounter in Otherworld.

A year and a day later, she is transformed into a beautiful lady, revealing that he had been tested, and from then on they lived in joy together. Did she actually change or did he see her inner beauty, the beauty of her spirit? When working with the Other People, sometimes things are not quite what they may seem, but are instead a test to see how you react—to see whether you only look at the surface or if you look deeper.

Many people, myself included, notice that when there are Fair Ones visiting, shiny things tend to disappear, especially keys when you need them. Communication is all that's required to have things you need returned, although they may show up in places you know you would never have placed them. Simply say out loud something like this:

I hope you enjoyed using the _____
(missing object), but I really need to have it back
now, so could you be so kind as to put it where
I can find it? You can borrow it again later.

With objects that you don't need immediately, say:

I hope you enjoy using the _____.
Feel free to return it whenever you like.

With the latter, I had a ring go missing for several months, then it turned up again in plain sight in my jewelry box, which I had actually emptied out when initially searching for it. I figured they needed the energy of the stone for some reason and was happy to share. Not being too attached to material things is beneficial for good Otherworld communication and connection.

The Energy of Words

People who move energy for magical works understand that words have power. Words can inspire, they can embarrass, they can create, and they can destroy. Because they convey the energy of the speaker, the rules still apply, so you can substitute "words" for "the Power" to be: "Do not use *words* to harm another, for what is *said* comes back." Balance is one of the unspoken rules of magic. "As above, so below" is familiar to most practitioners of the Craft, but it goes beyond above and below so that there is always balance. If you feel that someone is slighting you or demeaning you with their words, you can take that energy and turn it into something positive for yourself. The problem a lot of people have with negative words directed at them is that they give away some of their own personal power by allowing the unpleasant words to have an impact on their emotional or mental state. You could envision the words rebounding on the sender with a flash of bright white light that shields you, or you could simply reverse the meaning in your own mind. Part of this involves developing your own self-confidence, being able to evaluate criticism objectively, and looking at the source of the unpleasant words. People sometimes use harsh words to reassure themselves that they are important, when in reality they feel very insecure. Other times they may sincerely seek to offer insight but are clumsy with their wording or tone. Evaluate the message and decide what you desire to do with the energy.

When using words in magic and Faerie communication, the meanings are important. Most people will say, for example, "I want..." or "I need...," but these words have multiple meanings, one of which is "lack" or "don't have." That is why I have been using the word "desire" when I talk about asking the Universe for something. I also suggest saying, "Manifest for me...." when asking for something, be it a better job, a promotion, an opportunity, and so on. Remember that "I want" simply means "I lack," while "I need" simply means "I don't have," and the Universe may respond with a shrug, "So?" You have not actually made a request; you have only stated your current condition. I recommend not getting too specific. You can express a general desire, and with an expectation that the Universe will know how to handle the matter, you leave

Do not use words to harm another, for what is said comes back.

the details in the hands of the Divine, as they know what is best for you. Love and Trust are not turned on and off but are a constant. A person once told me about requesting a partner and going into meticulous detail, but when the person turned up, the result was not satisfactory and no relationship came of it. There was a lesson in this experience: you have to *trust* the Universe, the Goddess and the God, to do what is right for you, so don't get carried away with exhaustive details.

Another aspect of words is that the Other People are not able to lie. This means that the words they speak will always be the truth, so to exhibit good manners, you must not be disrespectful, insensitive, or keen to pry into matters that are none of your business. While being restricted to telling the truth might seem like a disadvantage, they do have other options. They can be silent or they can be deceptive by telling the truth. This is another secret of Faerie communication: when you lay two truths together, the human mind creates a bridge between them and sees them as connected. This means the person hearing two truths links them as relating to the same thing. Misdirection and hiding the truth behind this method can bring about a desired result. This technique draws disparate things together, and even if noted in passing that they are not the same, the connection is still made.

Another kind of deception through truthfulness involves remaining silent when commitment is not desired. This allows the other person to assume concurrence where there may not actually be any. Applying these techniques of the Other People in your own world is up to the individual, but it exists and is useful information to know when working with the Other People and with overly inquisitive people in this world. It is important to give people their space—not everyone wants to give you their life history, personal information, or express their private opinions to you, so be respectful and discreet rather than demanding and intrusive in your conversations.

In magical works, the spoken or written word gives direction to raised energy to achieve a goal.

In magical works, the spoken or written word gives direction to raised energy to achieve a goal. Think about what is desired and distill it into one or two words so that after stating your purpose for raising the energy, you can then send it on its way with an emphatic statement, followed by a conclusion such as "So mote it be!" or "It is done!" See the energy as departed and off to do the work requested, then put the matter out of your mind. Talking about, fussing over, repeating, or refreshing a spell casting simply drags the energy back until it becomes dissipated rather than releasing it to do the requested job.

With the four sides of the witch's pyramid—to know, to dare, to will, and to keep silent—the magical prohibition of silence prevents people from interfering with the energy you raised for a particular purpose, which is sometimes seen as the tip of the pyramid ("to go"), as in sending the energy raised to do the work assigned. Since words have power, telling someone you are going to do a spell to accomplish a goal can create an energy blockage. The person might not wish you well with your project for any number of reasons. If the person offers you discouragement or verbally diminishes your chances for success, this could indicate a problem of fear, rivalry, envy, jealousy, anger, or a desire to be in control.

If you must tell someone about your magical workings, wait until after the successful completion. Words that cast doubt in the mind of the magic worker dampen the aspect of "knowing it in your mind" and thus can throw up an energy roadblock. Avoid the whole issue by keeping silent until the results are achieved so you don't end up wasting energy trying to overcome someone else's objections or opposition to your plan. There are times, of course, when people of similar mind-set get together to do energy work, and the additional energy is very helpful, but be sure everyone is on the same page and dedicated to the stated result desired.

Rules for Communication

The rules for Faerie communication and connection are generally perceived as contradictory, which is typical of Otherworld. Some of these rules have already been touched upon, but I will elaborate on each. As always, things of Faerie may not be immediately obvious, so do not rush to judgement or presumption as you read these:

- To give is to get, and to get is to give (give a gift to receive a gift).
- Never reject a fairy gift.
- Never say "thank you" to the Other People.
- To gain a good friend, you must be a good friend.
- Do not use broom.
- Never burn magic-infused straw.

- Ask plants for permission in magical work.
- To win is to lose, but to lose is to win.
- To live is to die, but to die is to live.
- What you take into Otherworld is what you will find there.

To Give Is to Get, and to Get Is to Give

While this rule is closely related to the idea that you have to give a gift to receive a gift, it is also an injunction that creates an energy connection between giver and recipient. Think of it as when you go to a birthday party and give a gift, then when you have your birthday party, the previous recipient gives you a gift. This becomes a circle of compatible energy. If you have a spat and no longer exchange gifts, the energy cycle is broken.

When you give something to the Other People—as, for example, an offering—you are opening a channel of communication. This is a message to the Fair Ones that you would like to establish a relationship, and as such, it is their choice whether or not to respond. Not every invitation is accepted by humans, and the same applies to the Other People. By initiating this contact, you are awaiting a reply. Because they have good manners, you will very likely receive an answer, for as the recipient of a gift, the Other People will feel the need to bring the energy into balance. The degree of reciprocation will likely depend on how they interpret your mind-set and heart-set.

Gift giving engages energies in an exchange that creates an equitable relationship with the Fair Folk. The gift exchange binds the energies between you and the Fair Ones and your work if you are giving a gift to receive something for a magical project. This is why it is important to be certain that connection and communication is what you desire, for once you initiate contact, you open the door for an obligatory response of some kind, and you must be sensitive to that, but also grounded.

The nature of the gift is up to you. I once needed a pinecone for a spell but had nothing on me to give as a gift, so instead I drew a pentagram on the ground at the base of the tree from which I received the pinecone and gave it a blessing. The spell went fine, so I knew the gift I gave was appropriate. You can also create a circle of protection around a plant, offer a blessing, or offer milk, wine, beer, whiskey, water, grains, ginger, small shiny objects, coins, jewelry, ribbons, and so on. A beverage offering may be in a bowl or cup, or it may be poured upon the ground as a libation to the spirits of the land. The important thing is that when you seek something, you must first give something to initiate the energy cycle.

Never Reject a Fairy Gift

While this applies to the Other People, it does not apply to our human interactions. We are usually taught to accept gifts offered to us, but I will qualify that with the caution that you need to trust your instinct or intuition in this matter because among witches there are those few who become hungry for power and will use a gift as an attachment or means of insinuating themselves into the aura (natural energy field) of someone they seek to control or whose power they hope to siphon. Here is a "reality check" from decades of experience: not every gift is sincere. To decline a gift may result in a pretense of offense by the giver, followed by an insistence that the gift be accepted—rather like the poison apple repeatedly offered to Snow White until she took it and ate a bite. Energy traps exist, and you need to have your awareness up and know that your spirit guides and invisible helpers are close by to give you a helping hand. If you are not at ease receiving a gift, it is okay to reject it because if you receive, you give, and if you have nothing at hand for a gift exchange, it could be a portion of your energy that is removed to create balance. Gift giving can be sincere and genuine, but it can also be a means of asserting dominance or forcing a connection through an unexpected gift or one that is beyond the ability of the recipient to reciprocate with something of like value. This creates an energy imbalance, allowing the original gift giver a superior position in the energy cycle.

Fortunately, this is not the case when working with the Other People. A freely given fairy gift can be proof that something you did pleased the Other People or they are reaching out to you to see if you are interested in communication. As described earlier, this type of gift is something that you might find in your path or doorstep that has no reason to be there, or something that you asked for and received in response. I once asked during a meditation for some kind of evidence to confirm that an encounter I had with the Goddess was genuine. Afterwards, I went outside to the little dock behind the house, and there, just under the water's edge, was a large, shiny conch shell. This is a symbol of the Goddess, and I was overjoyed with the prompt reply. The shell had not been there in the morning, so I knew it was the affirmation I sought. I kept it on my altar for several decades until I found a place for it, along with a pair of antlers for the God, at the base of a statue of Diana centered in a ring of oak trees in my yard. Usually the surprise gift will be something familiar, but it could also be some other unusual object, so when you receive a gift from the Other People, remember you can praise it, express your delight at receiving it (and possibly why), what you intend to do with it, or how you will keep it until you understand how to use it, but, as follows in the next rule, NEVER say the words "thank you."

Never Say "Thank You" to the Other People

Over the past fifty years of giving instruction on working magic to individuals and to groups, I emphasize this rule and explain that to the Other People, a thank you is not only dismissive, but it is also perfunctory and changes the equal footing between you and the Other People. It shows that you are taking a gift and abruptly terminating the energy connection with the giver. "Thank you" terminates the communion and discharges the giver to go about their other duties, rather like when a server at a restaurant brings you your dinner plate or a cashier hands you change or even when someone lets you ahead of them in line. In human interaction the use of "thank you" is an expression of gratitude but not necessarily one of opening the door to lengthy conversation, making a new best friend forever, or doing anything else to reciprocate the initial action (except, perhaps, leaving a nice tip for the server). While these words are polite in certain human conditions, saying thank you to someone who gives you a birthday present without words of praise or expressions of delight can also be deflating to the gift giver, leaving the person to wonder if the gift was really liked or appreciated.

The Other People are all about energy flow, and working with them takes an awareness of the subtle nuances of language and the energy of words. Abruptly cutting the energy link between the giver and receiver of a gift with a "thank you" is considered rude in the sense of coarse manners and will end not only the energy exchange, but also the magic. If you slip up and say the forbidden words, apologize at once or qualify the mistake, such as following up with a hasty, good-natured, "...meant really as a sincere expression of my appreciation for..." This may help mitigate the inappropriate earlier T.Y. words and re-weave

Saying "thank you" will not only end the energy exchange, but also the magic.

the energy connection. The real importance of not saying "thank you" is that by saying it you sever the energy connection between you, the gift, and the giver. But by praising the item for its attractiveness, usefulness, or magical energy (as perfect for your magic space, your staff, or stang), you extend the energy contact, and it will remain there to energize any magical purpose in which it is later used. It is through the gift that you have an open line into Otherworld and the Other People, whereas the "thank you" is like hanging up the phone: end of conversation.

The result of cutting off the energy connection and ending the magic is found in the old fairy tales wherein a gift of gold that is thanked turns into dry leaves the following day, but when a gift is praised, the energy remains and brings the recipient good fortune in life. When you say you will put the gift in a keepsake box until such time as you know how to use it, you are acknowledging that the Other People already know the time will come when the gift will be put to work, that you will have it when you need it, and that you trust the decision of the giver to bestow it on you in preparation for when you will need it. By not severing that energy cord, you retain that energetic assistance from Otherworld with Perfect Love and Perfect Trust.

Along with the traditional admonition against saying "thank you," I am adding do not say "please." This insight came from my previously mentioned conversation with the green dragon. Humans are taught that *please* and *thank you* are the magic words, and they may well be in our daily interactions, but they can also be poisonous depending on the person's tone and delivery. A sharply spoken "please" is insulting; a haughtily spoken "thank you" is condescending; a tersely spoken "thank you" is insolent; a drawn out "please" is a childish and whiny demand, usually for something you should not have; and a wistful "please" is, as the green dragon cautioned against, groveling and therefore insulting to someone who had thought better of you. Since the Other People are acutely aware of nuances in speech, it behooves you to speak with respect and in friendship with positive self-confidence. Otherworld is not a place for the energies of timidity or arrogance.

Otherworld is not a place for the energies of timidity or arrogance.

While it is good to appreciate the little moments of connection we experience, allowing us to recognize that we are part of something larger and interacting with the deities and Other People, try to avoid becoming addicted to confirmations and validations. Once you have actually met the Divine or the Other People, it will remain in your memory as a singular moment of joy and transcendence. If you keep trying to revive that sensation, you are more likely to cause them to take a step back for your own psychological and physical well-being. The old stories remind us that getting too wrapped up in the connection can lead to a person becoming listless, suffering from melancholia, or pining away and eventually giving up on life. We are here for reasons we set between lives, and getting diverted by wistfulness is not healthy. A more casual approach should be engaged in, such as by seeing the deities as divine parents who watch you grow, or the Other People as friends who drop in now and then but are not becoming tenants or landlords.

To Gain a Good Friend, You Must Be a Good Friend

This rule is appropriate whether you are actively seeking an Otherworld companion or you are looking for connection and communication without commitment. Not everyone who works with the Other People desires a personal friend but is instead happy to work alongside nature spirits and the Fair Ones for the energy they offer to those who respect and honor them. Going beyond this to gaining a friend can be accomplished by extending an invitation through a ritual such as the companion quest or by accepting an invitation extended to you by one of the Other People.

The invitation extended to you may be subtle, perhaps with the finding of special gifts. By accepting the gift, you are creating an energy link, the strength of which might depend on the nature of the gift. For example, finding a crystalline or fluorite palm-sized stone in which you see someone looking out at you or a scene unfolding within may be an invitation for friendship, while finding a tiny stone cup and a plain gold ring may be an offer of marriage, so although you accept the gift, it is important to know how you choose to use it. Turning the palm stone into a portal, for example, offers you companionship wherever you go with the stone. With a marriage offer, you should take the time to contemplate the matter or simply use the gifts as tokens of connection to Otherworld rather than sip anything from the cup or wear the ring. The ring is still traditional in our world, and the cup used to be a common part of the marriage ceremony, with each person taking a sip from the "loving cup" to signify the marriage is mutually sealed. Today it is more likely to be seen as part of the wedding reception activities. If these particular gifts are accepted, utilizing them as tokens or symbols of Otherworld indicates that you have gained a friend. Drinking from the cup and wearing the ring will likely cause the items to disappear unexpectedly, to be kept safe in Otherworld. Since this means that you have gained not only a friend but a partner who will be devoted to you and watch over your well-being in this world, consider your options carefully, for when you depart this world, you can expect to be welcomed into the Otherworld.

Do Not Use Broom

Broom is a shrubby plant whose spears of yellow flowers have an intense dusty aroma that the Other People find offensive, so if you are seeking to attract them, do not plant broom on your property. There could be other reasons for their distaste for broom, perhaps due to the association of sweeping energies along with entities from a ritual circle or even as a sign of respect for the association of the besom in practice, but not one made of broom. A witch's besom should be made of straw or local plants used to create brooms, such as palmetto leaves, palm fronds, corn husks, sorghum tassels, or the twigs of various trees such as birch and willow. On a camping trip during a full moon I found a pine needle–covered twig that made a perfect besom. Indeed, having arrived without any of my tools, all that I required was provided by Nature at my campsite, including small chunks of wood naturally shaped that I used to represent the Goddess and the God, and at a different campsite I found stones nearby that were perfect for their representations.

While there are different varieties of broom plant, and they are beneficial for combating erosion, you will need to trust your intuition if you are set on having these showy evergreen shrubs in your yard. If the aroma of a variety of broom is particularly strong, you may prefer something a bit more subtle. There are broom varieties with flowers of golden yellow, orange, red, and combinations.

Never Burn Magic-Infused Straw

I recommend extreme caution if burning straw since it can be used as a temporary residence by a fairy or as a fairy steed. If you must burn straw, first say you are going to burn it and then shake it up so that any entities within know to depart. Straw can be used as a temporary residence for a fairy called upon for protection or aid in magical work. I used to ensure uninterrupted rituals in my home by calling a fairy into a bit of straw:

> *I call upon the Fair Folk to send someone*
> *to inhabit this straw and guard my door so*
> *that my rites are not interrupted.*

I would then set the straw in the entry hall, pointed at the front door. When my ritual or magical work was completed, I removed the straw to the yard, waved it as I bid my guardian farewell with a blessing, and released the straw to the wind (elemental Air).

Ask Plants for Permission in Magical Work

When asking a plant for permission to use part of it, you should tell it what you need and why. The plant can then offer you a portion, withdrawing its spirit but leaving the plant energy to aid you in your work. Look to see what part appears brighter or more attractive to you, or what part shines or moves, to know what you can take for your use. With herbs usually you will snip or pinch off the topmost portions just above a leaf cluster to encourage new growth. With roots you can separate a piece and replant the rest—this is especially easy with plants like ginger, whose roots can be separated in fall and replanted for new ones to grow in spring. If the plant says no, you must respect that and think of a substitute or ask a different plant. Sometimes a plant is not ready to be used (like the mugwort I asked), while other times the plant knows you need something weaker or stronger for your magical work. You may find that the image of the appropriate plant springs to mind, and you can trust this telepathically received information.

When you take a sprig, flower, nut, seed, or root, be sure to first give the plant a gift, as detailed earlier, and include fertilizer or water in order to establish a reciprocal relationship with the plant. People who garden will often feel attached to their plants, sympathizing when there's an attack of aphids, bringing ladybugs to the rescue, providing shade, sunlight, and whatever else is needed for the plant to be healthy and thrive.

Part of this relationship is knowing when is the best time for you to harvest produce or herbs from a plant and remembering to first ask permission. When you plan to add an herb to burn in a consecrated candle, for example, you first call upon the indwelling plant spirit to show you which portion you may cut for your work, and you give a gift to bind a voluntary bit of the energy necessary for the magical intention. When you add that cut portion to the spell candle, you call upon the plant's energy, such as with "I call upon you, rosemary, for good health!" then add it to the candle flame and thus release the energy to accomplish the purpose of the spell. The plant also benefits by letting its energy serve a greater purpose, connecting with the energy of the magic worker, and in this way the plant increases its own spiritual light.

To Win Is to Lose, But to Lose Is to Win

Winning and losing in human experience is about competition and dominance. When you win, you show dominance, but when you lose, you show failure or relinquish previous dominance. But with the Other People, energy in balance is optimal, not dominance or submission. This rule is difficult to explain, but it can be felt empathically. When you make a connection with Otherworld, being "in control" will limit your experiences to what you already know. Releasing that need to be in control will allow you to access new insights and make new friends. That is why, although a winner in a competition will shake the hand of the loser, the winner can only feel self-pride at the expense of hurting the self-esteem of someone else. The loser, however, can feel satisfaction from knowing they did their best and did no harm to the other person, but are actually the one responsible for the winner's gains in self-esteem.

So, the loser is the winner because the winner needed the loser to feel a winner, and the winner is the loser because the loser provided the means for the winner to feel successful.

In essence, winning and losing works energetically in reverse. You can only win if someone else loses, which takes away some of your spiritual light, and when you lose, you have gained spiritual light by helping someone else achieve their goal. This is the hidden message behind turning the other cheek—not defiance or submission, but actually allowing the aggressor to release more spiritual energy into the target of that aggression. In sports, the poor winner is normally decried, but the good loser is held in esteem. These are internal empathic assessments made by the spirit within each person relating to the spirit within others, for we are all connected through Spirit.

To Live Is to Die, But to Die Is to Live

This is a rule that may indicate why the dead are often conflated with the Other People; however, it is not a contradictory statement so much as one indicative of energy balance. There is a belief that it is possible for one of the Other People—be this an elf, dragon, or other denizen of Faerie—to die deliberately in Otherworld in order to incarnate as a human in this world, for whatever reason, only to live that life, die, and return to Otherworld and resume their former identity, and thus restore the balance. The idea of starseed children (human children born in this world after dying on another planet) echoes this concept.

From a human perspective, we are naturally born dying, for that is what our bodies do whether through accident, disease, or aging. But this rule also reminds us that death is not a state of being, it is a passage, or transition, from the state of physical being into the state of incorporeal being. People may become interested in spirit communication for verification or validation of their belief that the spirit really exists and that there really is an afterlife with a continuation of one's consciousness. On the other hand, scientists and psychologists tend to be skeptical without empirical evidence, but they expect evidence of the numinous to come from the physical.

Another aspect of this rule is found in what is called the shamanic death. This is when a person has the vision or dream experience of dying and returning from this death with knowledge for healing others or helping the dying to transition peacefully by removing the obstacles people place before themselves. When lifetime transgressions are absolved or forgiven, a dying person can move calmly into the afterlife. It is when they are not forgiven or when they cannot forgive themselves that the transition may be difficult or even halted. I have had spirits come to me at night fearful of moving on because of their lifetime's wrongdoings, but just giving spirits a blessing and the reassurance that the light awaiting them is pure love can help them to move on. If spirits do not feel secure enough to depart, I recommend giving them tasks to help them feel they are accomplishing something beneficial. I have suggested to reluctant spirits that they guard the boundary of my property from unwanted intruders, and off they go.

My own shamanic death took place in a dream state with my spirit guide beside me. I was fearful of the situation I found myself in and I died in that dream, but then my spirit guide took me by the hand to stand again, released my hand, and stood to one side as the whole situation replayed, only this time I responded with calm confidence, overcoming my fear and not dying but instead gently bringing the situation under control. It is commonly said that if you die in the dream state, you will actually die in the physical state, but this is how the shamanic death happens. It can be spontaneous, come through a vision quest, or be accomplished through a tribal ritual or a ritual like the one presented earlier for opening the way, not just opening the door to communication with the deities and all beings but removing the door completely.

The concept of death passage and rebirth is one found in nearly all spiritual paths and religions. While explained or described in such a way as to appear unique to each path, it is actually part of an ancient tradition of human esoteric spirituality that can be traced at least to Neolithic burials with grave goods and red ochre on the remains. Knowing that spirit communication, divination, shamanic death, and OBEs may afford a connection to the Otherworld is why these subjects are studied and practiced by those who are seekers of the Old Ways.

One important aspect of the shamanic death and of travel to Otherworld is that there is a real danger that you may choose to remain. This means that you would give up this world for that world, leaving people here in pain and grief, while also not living up to your potential here or doing the work you had intended here when you were between lives. The allure may be strong, especially for teenagers, to remain with the spirits or the Other People, but that could bring great harm to family and friends left wondering what they could have done to prevent their loss of you. If you are not grounded and make such a journey, the Other People or your guide will likely obstruct your travel.

Part of living a magical life is appreciating your body as the temple of your spirit.

Never attempt any connection with Otherworld or spirits if you are not feeling grounded and self-confident, for you could find yourself tested as to whether to live here or not. The choice may be yours to make, but that doesn't mean your hosts expect you to take up residence with them any more than you would expect a friend to move in with you after sharing a dinner! Common sense must prevail, even in Otherworld. Sticking around where you have not been asked to remain is an imposition. Recognize that having an experience of connection is something to treasure and remember whenever you have doubts, but it is not something to extend without consideration for them as well as for the people in your life here.

I once was swept up in a beautiful dance with a wonderful, loving spirit in another dimension, and I would have liked to stay in that bright light and amazing flowing music, but I heard a sound of grinding mill-stones and I knew this was a signal that I needed to return to my body.

Part of living a magical life is appreciating your body as the temple of your spirit, the home that works tirelessly without your having to direct it, just to provide you with lodging. The cells do their work, and the muscles, bones, organs, lungs, veins, and arteries are all coordinated to keep the house functioning. If nothing else, you owe your body gratitude and protection from things that would imperil it, and you should work together in harmony for mutual well-being and survival. I knew that I could stay, but I also knew that I had to return, for we all have obligations. That is part of taking responsibility for our actions and choices. I returned, but I retain to this day the memory of that dance from when I was a teenager. I feel that I was allowed that opportunity to sample the beauty of another world because my spirit guide trusted me to make the proper decision.

What You Take Into Otherworld
Is What You Will Find There

The last rule is a hidden rule, which I have mentioned earlier and touched upon at different points. Your mind-set and your heart-set has a direct influence on your experience, so it is important that you enter with love and trust, but not with preconceived notions of what you will find there. If you insist on viewing things through a filter of your own creation, you deny yourself the joy of their reality. Setting your preconceptions aside and simply letting Otherworld and the Other People be as they are will give you a more fulfilling experience, and by not creating roles for them to play, you honor the Other People for who they are, and they will return the compliment.

Before entering into communication, make sure that you are in a good frame of mind and heart—not stressed, not upset, not worried, not fearful, but open to meeting some new friends and trusting that you will be received with kindness and consideration. Be confident and receptive, choose your words with care, and be respectful, for you are in their world and you are seeking to gain their friendship but are willing to accept their decision in the matter.

Playing with Glamour

One of the characteristics of the Other People is that they can change their appearance. This is part of a Faerie trait called glamour (sometimes glamoure), a word derived from *grammar*, which in medieval days was a book of magical practice called in French a *grimoire*, while *gramarye* is the Scottish word for magic. Glamour is more familiarly used as the term *glamor*, indicating the magic and enchantment that make a person particularly attractive. Today the word implies makeup, hair styling, high fashion clothing, and celebrity, as with a person who is glamorous, or "trending." In tales of Faerie, the meaning is to make something appear as something else, to disguise or to transform one thing into another, or even to make something invisible.

In magic, glamour is a type of covering, like a cloak of energy that transforms or conceals.

There are stories about sumptuous Otherworld banquets that, when viewed with eyes dabbed with church holy water, turn out to be nothing more than leaves and roots. Well, lettuce, kale, mustard greens, beets, turnips and turnip greens, various types of squash, wild rice, parsnips, cabbage, potatoes, and carrots are in that category, but at the time of these "revelations," meat and bread were the main foodstuffs for humans, with the addition of turnips and beets as peasant foods. Healthy vegetarian foods are apparently the mainstay of Otherworld cuisine, possibly including vegetarian "meats" such as can be found in grocery stores today for people who prefer a vegan diet. Otherworld feast halls are also revealed by holy water as not beautiful structures but dank caves or underground dwellings. Is this the reality? No, but for good manners, if you think holy water will reveal something unpleasant, the Other People will provide what you expect.

Another glamour trick played on humans in the old tales involves making leaves or pebbles look like gold, so that when a greedy person demands gold from an encounter with one of the Other People, the person is appeased by getting what was required. Once the gold is taken home or buried for safe keeping, it returns to the original form. But how does glamour really work? In magic, glamour is a type of *covering*, like a cloak of energy that transforms or conceals someone or something.

Many years ago, I was doing tarot readings for a charity along with several readers when I heard one of the crowd directors call out that there was a reading for me, and another person said I was in the back room with the other readers. The organizers were also back there taking the money and handing out tickets, so I said to them that I was going to play a trick on the director by becoming invisible. Their expressions showed their skepticism. I placed my hands above my head, and with the thought that *the person does not see me*, I ran my hands down a few inches off the length of my body, like covering myself with a cloak, and sat still. The director entered the room frantically repeating "Where's Ann?" while looking around the room and even right at me. The director's spouse, who was one of the organizers, began laughing, and I ran my hands the opposite way, removing the energy cloak, resulting in a startled cry of "Where'd you come from?" The couple were still laughing about this episode fifteen years later.

Glamour can be applied in other ways, as with protecting your car while driving down the highway. When another vehicle gets too close—tailgating—you can quickly envision a shield of energy wrapping around the car starting from the center of the underside, up the front, over the top, down the back, and back underneath, connecting where you began—this should only take a moment of thought, so you may have to practice this when you first sit behind the wheel, perhaps mentally associating the process with a sound like a ping. Next, visualize your car as having very long sharp quills, like a porcupine, laid close to the car's body, then like that animal, your car suddenly raises the quills. I have taught this technique in a class and a student told me at the subsequent class that when tried, it worked and the tailgating car had quickly backed off. If the quill imagery doesn't work, re-envision the energy as long, sharp swords being thrust out the sides, back, or front of the car as needed. As usual for magical work and moving energy, you must feel and know that it will work for this to be successful. If you have cars crowding yours on either side, just see your car's quills or swords jutting out all around it. Once the offending cars have backed off or moved more to the center of their lanes, you can retract the quills or swords. If they come close again, repeat the process. I have found that cars will normally keep their distance after one glamour visualization, but they'll definitely do so after two.

In another sense, glamour is something that might explain why there are so many conflicting descriptions of the Fair Folk, ranging from tall, beautiful, radiant beings to short, peculiar, bestial beings and everything in between, as can be seen with the amazing fairy art of Arthur Rackham. The Other People will present to you what you expect of them, so if you have biases against them, they will comply because, really, it doesn't matter to them what humans think of them. Good manners provide their guests with what is expected, rather like accommodating the different food and beverage preferences of the people you invite to a party. The Other People will know instantly the images you associate with them and fulfill your expectation. How do they actually look? Perhaps pure energy or brilliant light, but they are not us, and we are not them.

Spiritism and Spiritualism

Communicating with spirits is part and parcel to Fairie connection and interaction. There are many cultural traditions that connect the dead with the Other People, and I reiterate that the concept of Summerland may be either close to Otherworld or even part of it. I grew up with spirits coming and going in the household. My mother would speak to them and help them along their way or let them know she appreciated their assistance. On one occasion when we were fifty miles apart, she was using the Ouija board with a family member, talking to her spirit guide, when her guide stated, "There goes _____ (my father's guide)," followed by "There goes _____ (my guide)." My mother put away the board and telephoned me to see if I knew what was going on. I told her that I had felt the exchange of guides, but I did not know why my guide left in such a hurry. Later that day my father told us that when he was alone at his desk in his company office, he experienced a sudden sharp pain in his chest that immobilized him, but then the pain left, so he never called for help. His guide had called on a stronger spirit for help, and that was what my mother's guide reported on the board.

When we used the board, the spirit guides always spelled things out rapidly, even creating their own abbreviations for things. We learned names with which to address them, past life information (which for my guide I was later able to confirm), past connections, and even that a spirit guide can call on another spirit to be a guide for someone. My father was a convivial skeptic, but after what appeared to have been a mild heart attack, he never questioned that there were spirit guides. My mother always said that the spirits are good. No equivocation, because *all* have a portion of Divine Spirit within, differentiated only by their individual degrees of light, and thus energy.

I am not advocating the use of a spirit board since so many people have tainted the practice with their own fears, but if you choose to use one, consecrate it through the elementals to be a tool for your use by sprinkling it with salt (Earth), smudging it with white sage or incense smoke (Air), passing it through a candle flame (Fire), and sprinkling it with your own blessed water (Water); the latter may be saved from a previous sabbat or esbat ritual, or made during the full moon with your usual recipe.

> *I consecrate this spirit board to my use through the*
> *power of the Goddess and the God and the elementals*
> *Earth, Air, Fire, and Water. So mote it be.*

After each board session, give a verbal farewell and blessing to the spirits, slide the planchette off the board, and set it aside upside down.

Close the doorway by stating:

This session is now ended. Depart in peace,
all spirits who have come here, and my
blessings take with you. So mote it be.

Pass the smoke of incense or smudge over the board:

In the names of the Goddess and the God, with love
and respect, this space is cleared, and all the gateways
that were opened are closed. So mote it be.

The smudge is generally white sage, while the incense can be frankincense, dragon's blood, or sandalwood.

Store the board resting on its edge, not flat, separate from the planchette. Never leave a planchette on a board as this may invite a passing spirit to hang out and possibly play with a person's fears or insecurities.

A smoothly moving session comes about when the participants' energies are in alignment, so it may take several sessions before gaining satisfactory results, and it may be necessary to remove people out of a session or rearrange the sitting to get good results. The proceedings are usually monitored by one individual together with that person's spirit guide. To answer questions, a spirit guide may gather the information from other spirits present, access the Akashic Records, or call a spirit to the board who can give a knowledgeable response. People may act as channels while the guide helps direct the activities, so there may be times when the answers come directly into the mind and the planchette glides out the words. The more you connect with Otherworld, the more likely you are to find an increase in spirit contact as well, so be prepared to take this as a matter of course, without drama or alarm.

Usually spirits are felt rather than seen, but after being open to them, they are likely to become visible in a psychic sense, sometimes even as apparitions that can be photographed. If you find a spirit's manifestation fearful, you can ask it to change or simply give what aid you feel it needs and it will usually be on its way. I once had a spirit arrive looking like a decaying corpse until I reminded the young man that he could look as he did at his best. His appearance immediately changed, and I helped him to move on. What surprises me most about spirits is that many do not know how to move on or are so fearful of doing so that they need a blessing, reassurance, and a helping hand to remember that the divine light is pure love.

In one of my classes I decided to try a Ouija board experiment with those of my students who were willing. One student was particularly empathic, and to my delight we were able help the spirit of a child become reunited with his mother and she took him into the light. The energy in the room went from heavy to what I can only describe as blissful. Only two other students saw or felt the child and mother reunion, but everyone in the class was aware of the sudden uplifting energy that momentarily filled the room.

When you are able to see and speak with spirits directly, the spirit board is not needed.

Seeing and hearing spirits may actually make the spirit board unnecessary, and this may be developed into mediumship, which can be called Spiritualism or Spiritism. There is a slight difference between Spiritualism—begun in Hydesville, New York, at the John Fox house during the winter of 1847 when mysterious tapping noises were found to be focused around his two daughters, ages eleven and fourteen—and Spiritism, created by Allan Kardec in *The Spirit's Book* in 1857. Spiritualism had an initial focus of proving that spirits exist through various phenomena such as table tipping, getting a spirit to move something, make a noise, tap once or twice to indicate a yes or a no in response to questions, and other such effects, usually at night in a dark room. Spiritism takes the existence of spirits as granted and focuses on direct communication between the material world and the invisible world inhabited by spirits through a spirit board, mediumship, or channeling.

Both versions of spirit investigation, which have pretty much blended together under the banner of Spiritualism, generally reject Paganism, preferring to adhere to standard mainstream religious perspectives with required prayers and iconography. Over time, Spiritualism has taken on the concept of an afterlife that allows for a realm where spirits can dwell and still relate with the corporeal world, but it does not yet fully accept the Spiritist concepts of evolving spirits (through which a spirit may increase its light), reincarnation, and a plurality of worlds, which might also allow for the Other People, spirit guides, and ascended masters. The Spiritualist views on spirit beings are in their own state of evolution, especially as Eastern and shamanic traditions become better known in the West.

In the Old Religion, spirits were always a given and remain so today, although occasionally viewed through the societal filter of mainstream religion. Spirit contact can be spontaneous, opened through ritual, experienced in the astral, or through mediumship, channeling, and use of tools such as tarot, runes, ogham, crystal balls, pendulums, or spirit boards to answer questions and provide information about various factors of the afterlife or provide guidance with decision-making. The dark room or night scenario are not required, and indeed there are many times that spirits turn up in the daytime. Sometimes they are visible; sometimes they are simply heard as a disembodied voice. I once said hello to an invisible spirit the cat had alerted me to in a room, and later in the day when I was in a different room, I heard a feminine voice say a return hello, and I had the distinct impression that a woman had walked past the doorway.

When I continued the Ouija board experiment during the class after the child and mother had departed, I saw a spirit standing in the entry to the room watching us. This was clearly an adult man, wearing a white shirt with the sleeves rolled up and black trousers held up by suspenders in an 1800s style. I sent a mental invitation and got the immediate yet amused mental response: "I ain't getting on that thing!" I said nothing about this, but after our session ended, I asked the student sharing the board with me if anything else had happened. The student recounted the same exact series of events, described the man, and spoke the response just as the spirit had, which made the other students laugh. When you are able to see and speak with spirits directly, the spirit board is not needed, so it is a personal choice. When connecting with the Otherworld, some students become very receptive to spirit communication, some require a bit of practice, and others choose to step back rather than experience it at all.

Spirits may appear as orbs, faint outlines, people whose forms may be partially visible, people whose attire and facial expressions are apparent but you are able to see through them, or even fully formed and solid looking. While you might see a spirit, this does not mean that people around you will see them. I had four teenagers come into the shop near closing, wander around, buy some incense, and leave, but I only counted three going out the door before locking it up for the day, so I checked all the rooms and no one else was there. I asked a family member if they had seen the fourth teen leave, and I was told there had been only three. The fourth was so distinct that he looked totally alive to me, down to the details of his clothing, so I expect he was associated with one of the teens as a deceased friend or relative. Another time while I was sitting on a bench in a hallway during a Halloween event at a historic hotel, I saw a distinguished woman walking toward the party, pause, and look right at me. I smiled and nodded at her, and she graciously nodded back before taking a few more steps and vanishing. I later identified her as a former owner from a nineteenth-century photo in another part of the building.

Because these kinds of incidents show that spirits have the ability to mingle with the living and can be transparent or solid in appearance, there can be times when you may not know the nature of the person you are interacting with until something alerts you, such as the person fading away in front of you. You could be in a group activity and discover that only one other person is aware of a spirit presence, and that validation may offer reassurance for you, but you are the best judge of when or if it is appropriate to mention the sighting to anyone. It is possible that having a casual attitude, rather than screaming or running away, makes it easier for spirits to associate with you, and since the Other People are often associated with spirits, it should not be surprising that opening contact with one will often lead to contact with the other. You may feel a sensation of strangeness in contact, but you should not feel alarm.

When having a small drum circle after hours one night in my shop, I noticed a group of spirits down the hall watching us and heard their conversation. Only one other person in the drum group saw them and broached the subject carefully to me later, asking "Was there something going on down the hall?" I reas-sured the person that there were four spirits observing us, three male and one female. The person gave a sigh of relief, then said there was conversation but nothing understandable and asked me if I could make out what they were saying. I replied, "One male asked, 'What are they doing?' and the female answered with a pleasantly surprised tone, 'They're *drumming!*'" I had the sensation that she found the activity delightful, and the drummer was thrilled to have witnessed the mysterious and numinous, along with a quick validation that it was real.

When you feel something unusual, trust your intuition and give a pleasant greeting.

Spirits can be ascended beings watching over you, teachers, messen-gers, guides who commune with you between lives to help you achieve your life goals, companions who assist you in your life travels, or departed loved ones protecting you. Because they are often associated with the Other People, there may be ties between spirits and the Other People in other dimensional forms. Along with this is the possibility that small fairies, the type that flit around in the air and are sometimes seen in pho-tos as leaving streams of light in their wake, may appear small here but not elsewhere. Photographed orbs are also connected to spirits, showing that form and size can vary. Spirits and the Other People can be large, small, distinct, or indistinct, but when you feel something unusual, trust your intuition, give a pleasant greeting, and continue with what you were doing. Not every encounter is immensely significant; some are simply spirits or Other People passing by, curious, or needing to borrow something until you ask for it back.

chapter
5

Faerie
Ritual Work

Circle casting is usually the first thing done in ritual work, ordinarily to create a secure and safe place that contains the energy you raise until you release it to accomplish the purpose for which it was raised, but it is also a confined space wherein a portal may be opened into other realms or dimensions for your magical and ritual work and closed again. In connecting with the Other People in ritual, for magical work, or for communication, you may utilize some of the traditional methods of magical work, setting up within the designated space your ritual arrangement, having all your needed tools and equipment at one spot, usually your altar, be it indoors or outdoors. The altar table for your tools and ritual focus may be placed at the center of the circle or more toward the boundary, as you prefer. The altar is usually set closer to and facing the west quarter, which is the direction most aligned with, or associated with, Otherworld. Traditionally, west is the gateway to Otherworld and the land of inspiration, although north is also acceptable as the land of wisdom. For a companion quest, which is covered in the next chapter, the altar is at the west.

Creating a Safe Space

To create a Faerie circle, you will be working a dual circle for balance, creating an interface between this world and Otherworld that will be bridged during the ritual, so keep your notes handy to prevent getting confused about the direction of each activity. You will be moving around the circle both deosil (clockwise/sunwise, *right way*, from Gaelic/Old Irish *deisiel, dessel*) and widdershins (or counterclockwise, *traveling back*, from German *widar* and *sinnen*).

You may create your blessed water using spring water and burdock root (instead of the usual salt) during the circle casting or you can use leftover blessed water from a previous Faerie ritual, such as the Midsummer (Litha) sabbat. I like to make extra to keep on hand for magical use and to shorten a ritual or have more room on the altar at a subsequent ritual. If you make blessed water under the full or dark moon, these can be stored in jars for later use. I label my waters with type of moon and date. Special lunar events are also noted, such as a "super moon" or "blood moon," for when there is a need for extra power. Violent storm and hurricane waters can also be collected in a bowl set outside and bottled for later use when you need swift and decisive action.

The circle is swept deosil with a besom that is not made from the broom plant (it can be most any other usual plant such as straw, birch twigs, etc.), the light between the worlds is called at the quarters widdershins to prepare a space between this world and Otherworld, the circle is cast deosil, some of the blessed water is sprinkled around the circle widdershins, incense is smudged around the circle widdershins, the elementals are called to secure the quarters deosil, and the work or purpose for the circle begins. At the end of the ritual or purpose of the circle, the elementals are bid farewell widdershins, the circle is smudged deosil, some of the blessed water is sprinkled around the circle deosil, and the circle is finally opened widdershins.

For all of this, take your time. Ritual, magical work, or crafting is not a race. In ritual, I use the traditional Craft words "So mote it be" as a statement at various points, and this is an affirmation that what has been said is accomplished, literally meaning "So must it be," rather like "It is done" or "So be it." You can change that as you like, and emphasis is up to you.

If you have a special room in your home reserved for your magical activities, this place will acquire an energy of sacred space after regular use so that there may be times when you go right to the altar and start your circle casting without sweeping. There may also be times when you feel comfortable doing some works without the preliminaries of circle casting, but trust your intuition on this. The function of the circle with regard to Otherworld workings is another matter as the purpose is to unite two worlds, create a portal, and, when the work is completed, disengage that union and close the door to keep the worlds in balance; thus, you should always go through the steps in order to achieve the desired outcome. Spontaneous connections when the Other People are contacting you are the exception, for *you* are not opening the portal, *they* are, and your response should be trusting so you can simply go with the energy flow.

Your response to the Other People should be trusting so you can simply go with the energy flow.

You may be surprised to discover you begin expressing your rituals in rhyming couplets. No matter how silly or awful (doggerel), speaking in pairs of sentences whose last words rhyme actually puts a rhythm into your magic work that helps open the way to Otherworld and carry the raised energy to manifestation. The more you work with the Fair Folk, the more likely you are to rhyme in your ritual speech. Try not to get so concerned about rhyming that you lose focus on your magical work—let it come naturally or from your own prepared script. This sort of speech tends to creep into everyday conversation, which can be annoying to people, so keep the rhyming under control.

Preparing the Faerie Circle

The full moon and the dark moon are both associated with Otherworld workings. The full moon is a time of manifesting magical works and setting out offerings for the Other People, while the dark moon is especially conducive for travel between the worlds, although you can use either lunar phase as your intuition directs.

The altar should be a comfortable-sized table that will hold all your tools and magical workings. If you do outside ritual, a portable table or large flat stone or tree stump make good altars, and you can set your items on the altar so you are facing west. The altar may be uncovered or have a cloth that speaks to you of Faerie (such as with a leafy or herbal pattern) or is gray, green, white, lavender, or purple.

If you use altar candles, the best colors would be gray (for going between the worlds), lavender (for purification and cleansing), or green (for Nature and the Other People), or an arrangement with these using two candles (for the Lady and the Lord) or three candles, with the central candle representing the Goddess and God as one, and a candle snuffer to extinguish these rather than blowing them out at the end of the ritual. If you have room, you can place statues that represent the deities as the King and Queen of Otherworld (such as Freyr and Freya or nonspecific god and goddess figurines) on either side of the table, with the three candles between them.

There should also be a gray "working" candle placed more toward the center of the table. This candle will be attuned to the magical purpose rather than to representing the deities, and it will be used for some types of Otherworld contact. If unable to locate a gray candle, use a white one. A short pillar or votive-style candle works well for this because it can be put into a small cauldron and herbs may be added to it. Just be sure the container will hold all the melting wax of the working candle. I use either a pottery cauldron or a bronze bowl for the working candle.

You will have your wand on the altar, and it can be made of elder, hazel, willow, ash, elm, birch, or hawthorn. Also, you will have your athame, which may be of jasper, obsidian, jet, copper, silver, or other metal, although traditionally iron is not used. Some practitioners prefer to only use the wand in Faerie ritual; the choice is yours. Have a cup with beverage (fruity or herbal) and something to eat, such as a cookie, biscuit, or type of bread, on a small plate. For Otherworld rituals, I like to use a fruited breakfast bread, raisin bread, or multigrain bread from the bakery.

Place a bowl of spring water and a bowl of cut-up or powdered burdock root on the altar to create blessed water.

For incense, burn something earthy (patchouli), herbal (rosemary), or floral (lavender), or use a smudge bundle of white sage. If you can find or make it, combination smudges such as white sage with lavender or rosemary work well.

Have a libation (offering) bowl on the altar containing a small amount of flower petals (calendula works well, as does elderflower). If you do not have flowers available, you can substitute with calendula or elderflower herbal teas, opening the teabag into the bowl.

You will need a small bowl or plate with some crumbled mugwort to drop into the pillar candle. If you like, you may place something at the quarters to represent the elementals, such as crystals, candles, or objects. I sometimes use a small stump for Earth, a feather for Air, a chunk of pumice for Fire, and a seashell for Water. You could also have a light-toned silver bell on the altar, but if not, then you will clap two or three times between segments of the ritual. At Shinto shrines in Japan, people clap twice to alert the deities that someone is addressing them and once after the petitioning. In India, there is a bell hanging by the entry that a person taps with one hand while entering a Hindu temple.

Place a pentacle close to the middle of the altar where items may be set on it for charging. The pentacle is usually a circular disk with the five-pointed star on it that could be made of wood or even a ceramic fired square tile having the star within a circle. This item not only represents Earth but manifestation, thus bringing something into reality. Besides wood or tile, it may be made of a metal like copper, nickel, or silver. A seven-point star disk, called a fairy star or elven star, can be used in place of the pentacle to represent the Otherworld and manifesting through Otherworld.

Once you have set up your altar so it is appealing to you and has all you need for your work, prepare yourself for ritual in your usual manner, such as taking an herbal bath or shower, wearing special attire used only for ritual, and/or meditating prior to engaging in the ritual. When it comes to magical work, your attire is intended to help you feel that something special is happening, but casual clothing can also be worn depending on how your mind-set is for the work to be done. With apparel, wear what works for you.

Circle Casting and Ritual

Sweep the circle space deosil starting at the west:

> As I sweep this circle, may it be cleared of any negativity
> and chaotic energies so that it is made ready for my work.

Light the incense and candles, clap or ring the bell, and announce that you are about to cast the circle to greet the Other People and seek the blessing of the Goddess and the God in their aspects of Queen and King of Otherworld. Take the lit gray (or white) working candle around to the quarters widdershins, raising it at each place as you call upon the light between—

> I call upon the Light between the Waters
> to illuminate and protect this circle.

> I call upon the Light between the Fires to
> illuminate and protect this circle.

> I call upon the Light between the Airs to
> illuminate and protect this circle.

> *I call upon the Light between the Earths*
> *to illuminate and protect this circle.*

—and return the candle to the altar.

This action prepares the space between the worlds that you will open at the altar. Raise your athame (or wand) at the altar and announce your intent:

> *I cast this circle, in the presence of the Lady and Lord*
> *of Otherworld, to be a place where the Other People*
> *may manifest and bless me, who am their friend.*

Point the blade at the west as you then turn deosil (from west to north, east, south, and back to west), saying and envisioning the circle as you cast:

> *Around me, above me, below me—as a*
> *sphere is this circle cast and consecrated so*
> *that only love may enter and leave.*

Create the blessed water for use in the Otherworld ritual by touching the athame to the spring water—

> *Spring water is the purity of the*
> *Lady and the fount of life.*

—and to the burdock root:

> *Burdock is the Lord's root of purification and*
> *protection. I bless both to be used in this circle in the*
> *names of the Queen and King of Otherworld.*

Set the water on the pentacle, drop three knife-tips of root into the water, and stir three times:

> *Through the Lady and Lord of Otherworld*
> *is this water cleansed and consecrated.*

Lightly sprinkle some, but not all, of the blessed water around the circle widdershins and return it to its original place on the altar. Take the incense around the circle widdershins, fanning the smoke with your hand or a feather as you go:

> *With this smoke the circle is purified and*
> *sealed so that it is a circle of power.*

You can dab a bit of the water on your forehead to consecrate yourself if you so choose:

> *I am consecrated in this circle.*

Use the wand to call upon the elementals deosil (west, north, east, south, and back to the altar in the west):

> *I call upon you, elemental Water, to attend this rite*
> *and guard this circle, for as I have fluids and emotions,*
> *I am your kith and kin. Hail and welcome!*

> *I call upon you, elemental Earth, to attend this rite*
> *and guard this circle, for as I have body and strength,*
> *I am your kith and kin. Hail and welcome!*

> *I call upon you, elemental Air, to attend this rite and*
> *guard this circle, for as I have breath and thought,*
> *I am your kith and kin. Hail and welcome!*

> *I call upon you, elemental Fire, to attend this rite*
> *and guard this circle, for as I have heat and vitality,*
> *I am your kith and kin. Hail and welcome!*

Back at the altar, with your wand, draw above it the symbol for infinity, the cosmic lemniscate (a sideways 8):

> *Welcome, elementals at the four quarters!*
> *Welcome, Lady and Lord of Otherworld! I stand*

between the worlds with love and power all around
me. I ask for your blessings so that I may commune
with the Other People in peace and love.

Greet the Other People with open arms:

Hail to the People of the Land of Mist. I send my
greetings and ask that you hear my call and let the
gateway be opened between us in this world and
Otherworld. In the names of the Lady and the Lord
do I call upon the Fair Ones in peace and love.

Open the portal at the altar by lifting the gray working candle over the altar:

As this light does shine brightly before me, so does
the light of Otherworld reach into this place.

Move the candle across the altar from right to left, then set it back down at the center and add a bit of mugwort to the flame.

You are ready now to perform any ritual relating to Otherworld and the Other People, such as a Faerie-oriented sabbat or esbat, a meditation, creating a craft such as a charm bag or black mirror, doing a black mirror meditation, consecrating a portal stone, or other activity, but *not* the companion quest as the preparation is different.

The Fairy Meal

Once your magical work is completed, you can bring the ritual to a conclusion and regain grounding and balance through the fairy meal, which is the beverage in your cup and the bread or cookies on the plate. In fairy lore, the food of Otherworld makes people pine away, for nothing in this world is as tasty. What you are eating here is the food of this world, and that helps to bring your awareness closer to normal energy.

Clap or ring the bell, then bless the meal:

*I know of my needs and offer my appreciation to that
which sustains me. May I ever remember the blessings
of the Lady and the Lord, who bring spiritual life
through the bounty of Otherworld so that all is created
in undying beauty. I honor the Lord and the Lady,
the Other People, and the inner beauty of the spirit.*

It is the inclusion of Otherworld and the Other People that makes this meal different from the usual "cakes and wine" of the regular esbats and sabbats.

You can use wand or athame to bless your beverage, touching the tip to the cup:

*The blessings of the Queen of Otherworld
enter into this beverage.*

Pour a little into the libation bowl containing the flower petals. Touch the tip of the wand or athame to the plate with the bread or cookie:

*The blessings of the King of Otherworld
enter into this food.*

Add a bit of the food to the libation bowl of flowers. Raise the cup for a toast:

*I honor the power and grace, beauty and strength
of the Lady and the Lord of Otherworld.*

Take a sip from your cup and set it back on the altar, then enjoy your ritual meal while taking a quiet moment for connection, so you can feel the closeness of Otherworld and the presence of the Other People. Speak with them as desired, perhaps asking for their presence in your home and property, for their counsel when you have need, for their assistance in bringing a spell or other matter into manifestation, or for their aid in removing from manifestation something not desired.

Opening the Circle

When finished with the fairy meal, clap or ring the bell, then hold your athame level over the altar:

> *Lady and Lord of Otherworld, Fair Ones of the Land*
> *Beyond, I am blessed by your sharing this time with me.*
> *Watch over and guard me; guide me here and on all*
> *my paths. I came in love and I depart in love. I honor*
> *the land where the spirit is nourished in song and joy.*

Raise the athame upright:

> *Love is the Law and Love is the Bond. Merry meet, merry*
> *part, and merry meet again! Let the gateway between this*
> *world and Otherworld close once more as I take my leave*
> *of the Other People in peace and love. So mote it be.*

Kiss the flat of the blade and set the athame on the altar. Lift the gray working candle, move it from the left to the right, set it back down at the center, and snuff the candle:

> *The gateway is closed.*

With hands open over the altar, offer the first clearing of the circle:

> *Beings and powers of the visible and invisible,*
> *depart in peace! You aid in my work, whisper in*
> *my mind, bless me from all realms and worlds you*
> *inhabit, and there is harmony between us. My*
> *blessings take with you. The circle is cleared.*

You may use your wand as you bid a simple farewell to each of the elementals at their quarters, moving around the circle widdershins (west, south, east, north, and back to west):

> *Depart in peace, elemental (Water, Fire, Air, Earth),*
> *my blessings take with you. Hail and farewell!*

Take the incense or smudge, fanning the smoke deosil around the circle from the west to north, east, south, and back to the altar:

> *This space is purified so that all energies, spirits, and entities return to their realms with my blessings.*

Sprinkle blessed water around the circle deosil from the west and offer the second clearing:

> *This space is cleansed by blessed water and the gateways are sealed. The circle is cleared.*

With the athame, open the circle widdershins (west, south, east, north, and back to the altar) and offer the third clearing:

> *The circle is open, yet the circle remains as the magical power is drawn back into me. The circle is cleared.*

Touch the flat of the blade to your forehead to return the energy inward, then touch your palms to the earth or floor as an aid for grounding and bringing yourself back into balance on this plane.

I like to include a benediction:

> *The ritual is ended. Blessings have been given and blessings have been received. May the peace of the Goddess and the God remain in my heart. So mote it be.*

There are three statements of clearing, as threes are traditionally used to conclude or bind in magical workings. While the candle was used to open and shut the doorway between the worlds, the first clearing empties the circle of those energies that are accessible in this world. The second clearing cleanses and seals the gateways. The third clearing relates to the energy you initially utilized in casting the circle, and in opening the circle, it is cleared away as that energy comes back into you. Your purified magical power remains available for the next time you call it forth.

Communication Portals

When engaging in communication, creating a ritual circle keeps the opening in place, so when using a portal, I recommend first casting the circle as already described before launching into a session. Making contact through a portal is a type of Otherworld ritual as much as celebrating Midsummer with an emphasis on the Other People. There are various ways to create a portal, and sometimes portals simply occur. When that happens, stay calm and enjoy the sights while continuing with what you were doing, for the random portal tends to appear and then dissipate if you go about your business. Portals can be found in objects through which we can connect with the Other People, such as a small gemstone that fits in the palm of your hand, a sphere, or a larger free-form stone. A black mirror is another object that functions well as a portal to Otherworld, as well as through time, as when exploring a past life or meeting ancestors.

Portals can also come in the form of clouds, occur in meditation, happen in ritual, or open up when scrying or performing a divination with tools such as tarot cards, runes, or ogham fews. Dreams can be portals, and so can natural locations on the earth such as caves, narrow passages through tall boulders, stone outcroppings, silent open spaces in forests, groves, canyons, mountaintops, and woodland pools, to name a few. When I speak of stones, I am referring to all varieties, be these semiprecious gemstones, quartzes, transparent or translucent stones, or opaque ones like calcites. Not all stones need to be clear to be good for scrying or for portals.

I have acquired a few physical portals and experienced intangible ones over the past few decades, and I have also taught workshops where students create a portal in the class or bring something of their own to turn into a portal and be consecrated and tried out during the class. Some easy portals to find are the gemstone palm stones, which are smoothly polished flat oval stones that you hold in your palm; gemstone soaps, called this by gemstone merchants as these are shaped like an oval bar of soap; and black mirrors, which you can easily make or which can be bought. Crystal skulls are another common portal, but a lot of people have reservations about working with skulls. These tend to be more of a direct line through a portal to an ascended master, spirit guide, or wisdom keeper in another location, be it another dimension or elsewhere in the Universe. With an object type of portal, you can use it whenever you feel the time is right or you have need.

Gemstone Portals

An old folklore tradition claims that fairies do not have internal souls, but keep their soul in a stone that they carry in their mouths. To me this is an oblique way of identifying stones as portals to Otherworld, while the idea of the stone being carried in the mouth shows that the stone is a method of communication. Since fluorite stones are associated with Otherworld, these stones make ideal portals. Any stone, however, can be a portal if you are initially able to see something in it. Stones that I have found to be portals include fluorite, quartz crystal, dolomite, seraphinite, labradorite, pietersite, obsidian, and lodalite (a clear quartz crystal with inclusions or on a matrix looking like a water bubble over a riverbed). Portal stones come in all sizes, so if the stone is small enough to hold in your hands, hold it and quietly ask it if there is anything within that you should be able to see. If the stone is too large to hold, then set it on a flat surface (on top of a stand or an appropriately sized pillow if it's a sphere) and look into it.

When gazing into a stone, notice the variations or patterns of its markings. If you don't see anything, look into a different stone until you find one that shows you a scene, animals, or people, or all of these together. The energy of the stone should feel inviting and friendly. You could look for stones in rock shops, metaphysical shops, or on your own walks in Nature. If there is something about the stone that draws your attention, whether it is the texture, the colorations, or the energy field, this is an indication that it is willing to work with you.

Greet the stone and ask it to show you something that you will recognize today, such as with: "Hello, is there anything you would like me to see?" Then look in the stone and see if there is a change in your perception or something that you had not previously noticed. Sometimes your scrying area is small; other times it is expansive, perhaps even taking up the entire stone. If you have already seen a place in the stone, note what you see and if it changes while you are looking into it. If an animal is present, see if you can identify it and discern the surroundings. If an individual is there, say hello and that you hope you are not intruding, but you are happy to see the person. Ask if the person would like to visit with you from time to time, and wait for the response. You might hear something in your mind or you might see the figure nod or smile at you. If the answer is affirmative, you will see this person when you use the stone. If the response is negative, you can tell the person that it was nice visiting, but you will leave the stone for someone else, then put it back where you found it.

Talking with stones may seem silly, but it's a matter of being open to the idea of communication.

Talking to stones may seem silly, but accepting the animistic and pantheistic view that everything is alive and everything has a bit of Divine Spirit within makes this quite reasonable. Many people tell me they have heard stones call to them or even tell them they are waiting for someone else to collect them. It is a matter of being open to the idea of communication. When you bond with your crystal, hold it in your open left palm at your heart level and place your right hand under your left. Project yourself into the crystal, seeing it as a crystal house or looking deep into it as you see the features around you within it. Feel the crystal's texture, temperature, atmosphere, and so on. Is there a sense of coolness or warmth? Do flavors come to mind? Can you hear a sound or a tone? Is there a pulse of energy? Move into the crystal to flow through the walls, feeling your energies united and bonded.

Depart by regathering yourself at the center and returning to your own body. Rest and take a few deep cleansing breaths, then ground any excess energy by touching the floor or ground. The crystal is now active, and when you hold it, your pulses will match. With a large crystal that is too big to hold, place it where you can gaze into it and follow the same procedure, placing your hands on either side or around it.

How to Prepare a Gemstone Portal

Once a stone has shown itself to be a portal, you can then prepare it to be programmed for your use. Because stones are generally mined, then taken to locations where distributors can buy them and later sold to retail shops, then to individuals who visit the shop, the stones can pick up a lot of extraneous energy and energy cords from the various people who have handled or mishandled them. People tend to want perfection from stones but fail to realize that each one is individual and "imperfections" are subjective. When I find a compatible polished stone that has a hole in it, for example, I see this as an energy portal. You can whisper your request into the stone or, if the hole is large enough, insert a piece of paper with your written request, a blessing, or other message for the stone to energize. A crystal with a chip or with inclusions is as good a portal as an unfractured or clear one; it all depends on how you relate to the energy of the stone and how it relates to you.

Both amethyst and selenite have a very high vibration and never need cleansing.

Due to all of the previous handling a stone normally goes through before you find it, you should give it a good cleansing by smudging with the smoke of white sage, lavender, or rosemary. Know if your stone can tolerate water—selenite and covellite will dissolve, for example—or if salt will damage it. There are many books about stones, and there is also information on the internet, so learn more about the stone before you cleanse it if you plan to use water or salt on it. For the most part, smudging with white sage is a safe process, as is placing the stone on a larger selenite or amethyst.

I have not used salt very much for cleansing unless the stone seems to want it. One stone I bought gave a sigh of relief when placed in a bowl of salt and covered with more salt. The process made me think of the stone enjoying a day at the spa! I later rinsed it off with water and set it on an amethyst bed (a chunk with a number of points), used rather like a drainboard. Amethyst beds are great for cleansing all on their own as amethyst has a very high vibration and never needs cleansing itself. Just to let it know that I appreciate its work, I may smudge an amethyst. Amethyst beds used to clear other stones should be at least semi-flat and with large enough points to support a stone being set on the points for cleansing. Be careful not to set a heavy stone on the amethyst points, only ones that are of a lighter weight. Selenite is another stone that clears and never needs cleansing, but it can be more fragile, so a selenite plate or bowl is more beneficial for clearing other more lightweight stones. For heavy stones that do not like water, smudging is the most beneficial method of clearing.

To cleanse a crystal or other stone not harmed by water or salt, use a clean container set on top of a pentacle on your altar. Pour sea salt to coat the bottom of the container, set the stone on top of that, and pour more salt over to cover and absorb chaotic or negative energies. You can keep it in the salt for three or seven days, then remove the stone and rinse it with spring water (bottled is fine). Toss out the used salt away from your dwelling or pour it into a bag you can place in the trash so that you don't retain the residue of whatever was absorbed by the salt.

After cleansing the stone, cast the circle and carry out a consecration ritual to attune the stone with your energies and charge it to work with you. Set the cleaned, dry stone on the pentacle and, with the athame raised upright in your right hand, touch the stone with your left hand and say something like:

I call upon the power of the elementals and the Lord
and Lady of Otherworld to empower this stone as
a portal to open the way between the worlds.

With both hands now holding the athame, touch the stone with the tip of the blade and feel the power pass into the stone.

Through the elementals, the Goddess, and
the God, this stone is consecrated.

Set down the athame, hold the stone near your third eye, and focus your mind on the purpose for which you desire the stone to work for you, which in this case is to be a portal stone.

This stone is charged to work as a portal for me
to see into other worlds and dimensions, for as
we are connected through the elementals and
are kith and kin, so is this stone connected to
me to aid me in my work. So mote it be!

Pass the stone through the symbols of the elementals:

In the names of the Lady and Lord, this stone is
consecrated and charged to be used by me, blessed
and empowered through elemental Water (sprinkle
and wipe dry the stone), elemental Earth (sprinkle
with burdock root and wipe off), elemental Air
(pass through incense smoke), and elemental
Fire (quickly pass through candle flame).

Set the stone on the pentacle and hold your palms over it:

This stone is focused to aid me in my work.
So mote it be.

After consecration, the stone may be placed in the light of the full moon and under the energy of the dark moon, but not in the sunlight if this will fade the color (as with amethyst) or if its purpose is for Otherworld connection as it is best to contact Otherworld in twilight. Store the stone in a pouch or cover with a black cloth when not in use.

When you communicate with a crystal of any type, visual imagery is the best way to project your intent, so as you speak to the stone, visualize what you desire. Expect the crystal to understand, remembering that everything is connected through Spirit. The crystal will bond with you and even become protective, actively defending you and repelling any attempt by others to influence it. The crystals you bond with will recognize you and shed "non-you" energies easily, and your crystals and stones will reach out to you when they sense your need. This is why sometimes you feel "drawn" to handle or carry one of your stones. It is also how a crystal or stone can attract someone it wants to work with, for bonding goes both ways. If you feel you need to give away one of your crystals to someone, be sure to confer with the stone and let it know your intention, seek its consent, and clear it of your own energy cords with the smoke of white sage.

How to Open and Close a Portal Stone

Now that you have a portal stone, keep it concealed until you choose to use it. Cast your circle and sit in the center facing west, or at the western side of the circle, and have the stone on a table or other flat surface in front of you. If the stone is a sphere, it will be on a cushion or some type of holder.

Pass your power hand across in front of the stone, right to left:

Let the gateway be opened.

Now you can hold the stone in the palm of your hand or cradle a larger stone with your hands. Focus your eyes and thoughts on the stone, asking it either in thought or with words to reveal what it is that you seek. Look at the stone and see if there is something that draws your attention. Even with larger stones or spheres, you can turn them around with your hands to explore any changes or images that are coming to you. If your stone is one in which you have previously seen a person, politely ask the person to come forward and communicate with you. When working with a stone, you may hold it up to your third eye, then gaze into it to see what comes to you.

Some stones have a particular focus, such as locations in this plane, Underworld, Otherworld, or alternate dimensions. For example, I have a labradorite that is used for Underworld and spirit communication, while a crystal ball containing cinnabar tends to show mainly volatile situations around the world—I tend to keep this one covered most of the time—and my fluorite palm stones are Otherworld portals, but an egg-shaped dolomite accesses an alternate dimension and a covellite sphere provides guidance.

You should be relaxed when you open a portal. With the circle cast, have a candle going and incense burning so you should feel comfortable. If you prefer to have soothing music playing, keep the volume low so it stays in the background.

Once you have completed your work, you need to close the portal. Waft some of the incense smoke across the stone and speak a farewell from your heart, such as:

> *With the aroma of incense do I give my blessing unto thee*
> *and receive thine unto me. I honor our time together.*

Now move your hand across the front of the stone, left to right:

> *The portal is closed until such time I seek to see*
> *with blessings given and received. So mote it be.*

Cover the stone, open the circle, and store the stone in a secure place or carry it with you. A portal stone need not be sealed with a pentagram unless you feel the need to do so because it is your personal contact and the stone may be viewed from any side or direction, so the position of the doorway may change each time you use it.

Black Mirror Portals

The companion quest is presented in the next chapter, but you will need to have a black mirror first. I prefer that it be one made by the user so that the work is personalized and contains the desired ingredients. Making the tool is a ritual in itself, and this is followed by being consecrated and charged. Besides being useful as a portal to Otherworld, it can also be used for scrying and meditations. While you can buy a mirror manufactured with actual black glass or made from obsidian, these tend to be costly and will not contain your magical work that opens gateways. I prefer to use a mirror that I have ritually made with all the components within it; however, a ready-made one may be consecrated and charged with the ritual that follows the construction instructions below.

When you cross dimensions, remember you are on someone else's turf.

The blackness of the mirror's surface opens the way to encounters and can be augmented by the placement of one or more candles. When used to open a door to Otherworld in a Faerie ritual, there is no guarantee that you will gain entry. Even if you open your own front door to a stranger, there is no requirement for you to allow the person to cross the threshold, and the same applies to Otherworld. If you have made the attempt and been unsuccessful, back off, rest a bit, and try a calming meditation before trying again. If you are still unable to get past the blockage, there may be some issue you need to resolve, some mind-set or heart-set that needs adjusting, so simply close the portal and take time to reconsider your goals and intentions, and release any preconceived notions that might be an impediment.

To me, the best plan is no plan, no agenda. Instead, you are knocking on the door, as it were, and waiting to see if you get invited to the barbeque out back. If not, depart with gratitude that the door was opened. Try again another time after making sure your spirit is comfortable and not overly excited. Why would someone be unable to make the connec-tion? Possibly because the Other People are aware that the time is not right or that contact would be a distraction to what the person should be doing. They could also know what the person expects is not feasible or they might notice that the person's energy field is not in alignment, and so on. When you cross dimensions, you are on someone else's turf, and sometimes jumping in is not appropriate. Remember to trust the decision of the Other People and wait for a better time.

Creating a Black Mirror Portal

A black mirror is really just a piece of glass with one side coated or painted to keep the light rays from passing through. Mirrors can be tall, short, round, rectangular, and so on, as well as concave or convex. My personal favorite is to make black mirrors from oval photo frames with an easel back of sturdy cardboard and turn buttons so the back can be removed, put back in place, and the mirror can be set upright on a table for use. When I conduct classes on the subject, I bring all the materials necessary for each student to create their own mirror during class, then we consecrate and charge them and give them a try. Although the mirror can be made in one sitting, there are other options for initially washing the glass and preparing it for being turned into a black mirror, so look over the directions and be prepared before you continue.

You will need a photograph frame with glass and an easel backing that opens up (not the slot type where a photo would be slid down), and you will need spring water.

Open the back of the photo frame by using the turn buttons and set aside the easel backing. Remove the usual paper oval advertisement or sample picture. Carefully pop out the glass and wash it with spring water—natural if you have collected this, otherwise bottled works. Dry the glass and let it sit in the moonlight during a full moon, seeing this as a time for bringing things into manifestation, magical power, and a time when the Other People are likely to be abroad. Set it out again during a dark moon, seeing this as a time for spirit contact, Otherworld communication, meditation, and divination. In this way, your mirror is attuned to both the light and dark aspects of the Divine so you can use it for successful connections, meditative explorations, and travels to other realms. Once the glass is ready, have all your materials together before you begin the process of making the black mirror.

To continue, you will need:

- wax paper
- black glossy enamel paint
- a paint brush with smooth bristles about an inch wide
- a black marker
- a black taper candle
- matches
- a pinch of each of the following herbs: mugwort, elderflower, and lavender (if you cannot get the herbs, they are often available as single plant herbal teas loose or bagged)
- the instructions copied out so you can move through the process with ease

The next stage is to paint the interior (back) of the glass with a glossy black enamel paint, a small can of which you can get in any store where paint supplies are sold. Be sure the label shows it is a glossy enamel. Use an artists' size brush with about a 1-inch width for even brush strokes. Lay the glass on wax paper and carefully brush on the black paint just on one side, making sure there are no streaks or bare spots. I recommend using your brush fairly loaded with paint, but you will need to find the right amount as you work. I tend to slop paint over the edges of the glass, which makes the glass stick to the wax paper, but the enamel paint peels off easily. Too little paint leaves streaks of clear in the glass, and too much will simply take longer to dry. The ideal is to let the paint dry completely in a dust-free area for a day or two, then take the glass off the wax paper and tidy it up around the edges.

To complete the mirror, have ready the black marker, a black taper candle you can hold, and matches (or lighter), and in separate piles in your work area a bit of each of the three herbs so you can add these to the mirror as will be indicated after creating the bindrune (more than one rune created like a monogram) that follows.

On a clean sheet of wax paper, place the frame face down and lay the glass in the frame so the painted side is up and unpainted side will be facing outward when the frame is later sitting upright. On the cardboard frame backing, you will draw with the marker symbols that will then lay against the back of the mirror and thus be hidden from view when the mirror is finished. Draw the following runes in the order stated, but as a single unit as illustrated, with each new rune adding new portions to the overall design or incorporating part of an existing rune.

Carefully draw each rune individually with a black marker, even when going over a previous line, as indicated in the series of illustrations after the rune list. Say the name of each individual rune—

Dayg

Sigh'gel

Ken

Tie ear'

Thorn

Ee' oh

—prior to drawing it on the backing, and say its purpose as shown below. For the first rune, you say, "Daeg for working between the worlds," and draw it. For the second rune, you say, "Sigel for wholeness and vitality," and draw it. Continue until all six runes are drawn in the order shown and you have one complete bindrune that looks like the final illustration, then set aside.

Daeg for working between the worlds,

Sigel for wholeness and vitality,

Ken for opening energy,

Tyr for success,

Thorn for protection,

Eoh for a channel opened and sigil bound.

This bindrune is a double triad for passage between the worlds and balance. The combination affords magical protection, seeing clearly, power, balance, and success, with the final rune tying it all together and providing the opening of the portal when instructed by the person using the mirror.

With the glass already in the frame and the backing nearby, it is time to add the herbs onto the back of the glass. Use ground-up dried mugwort, dried elderflowers (not berries, leaves, or wood), and dried lavender flowers (not leaves or stems). Make sure the paint is not wet or the herbs will come through and be seen from the front of the glass, which may interfere with the purpose of the mirror. As you say the words, scatter a small amount of the herb named across the painted side of the glass:

Mugwort for divination;
Elderflower for blessing;
Lavender for Otherworld and working with the Sidhe.
With blessings given and blessings received,
this mirror is empowered.
So mote it be!

Immediately place the backing with the bindrune over the herbs, and slip the turn buttons or clips that hold the backing onto the frame into place. Now take the black candle, light it, and carefully drop the melting wax along the edge of the backing all around the back of the frame to ensure that the back does not accidentally open. This seals the energy into the mirror.

Set up your altar materials at the north. The mirror may be used for a variety of purposes, and during those times it can be placed at the north or the west, but for a general consecration, set up facing north. Include a red working candle (a short votive style is fine) that will represent elemental Fire, a bowl of chopped or powdered burdock root for elemental Earth, lavender or patchouli or sandalwood incense for elemental Air, a bowl of blessed water for elemental Water, a pentacle for manifesting,

and a black cloth for wrapping the mirror. The mirror can be consecrated for your use in your usual manner or by the following:

Hold up the mirror in your hands:

In the names of the Goddess and the God,
I consecrate this black mirror to my use.

Then you will pass the mirror through the symbols of the elementals
one at a time as follows:

I call upon the elementals to charge this tool
through Earth (sprinkle the mirror glass
with burdock root and clean off),
through Air (pass mirror through the incense smoke),
through Fire (pass mirror quickly through the
flame of the working candle),
and through Water (dab the mirror glass
with a bit of blessed water and dry it).

Lay the mirror on top of the pentacle with the glass side up, hold your
hands with your palms upward above the pentacle, and say:

Through the power of the Goddess and the God,
this black mirror is charged, blessed,
and consecrated to my use.

Turn your hands palms downward over the mirror. Bring your palms
close to the mirror without touching it, pushing the energy into the mirror as you say:

So mote it be!

Wrap the mirror in a black cloth and set it on the altar or store as
desired until you are ready to use it. You may touch the floor or ground
if you feel you need to release excess energy.

The mirror should be covered with a black cloth when not in use. The
smaller type of photo frame can usually fit into a drawstring black cotton

or velveteen bag and be kept in a drawer or left on the altar. If using a larger mirror, you can simply cover it by draping a black cloth over it. The material is not particularly important, but something soft such as silk, cotton, or velour works well. This is like tucking the mirror into bed to sleep until you awaken it for your first use.

Using a Black Mirror Portal

When you use the mirror for the first time, set it up in the desired location (such as a table or altar area), prepare the place with the altar candles or working candle(s), cast your circle, light incense, and remove the covering. Without touching the mirror, activate it by gently sweeping your open hand right to left across the front of the mirror, seeing this motion as opening a door. Light whatever mirror candles you are using (more on that in the next chapter), depending on the particular purpose for opening the portal. You can have one on either side of the mirror or a short candle in front of the mirror or all three, depending on the use of the mirror. When your mirror work is completed, snuff the candles. Without touching the mirror, gently move your hand across its face in the opposite direction to close the door. With the idea of locking the door, draw with your forefinger a pentagram over the lower-right edge of the mirror and whisper into the mirror:

Covering your mirror with a cloth is like tucking it into bed to sleep until you awaken it.

The gateway is closed and sealed.

Cover the mirror at once with the cloth.

From now on, when you use the mirror, you will draw with your finger the pentagram at the lower-right edge and gently sweep your hand across the face of the mirror right to left, saying:

The gateway is open.

When your session is completed, close the gateway as described above. Think of the pentagram as the key that unlocks the door. When you first made or used the mirror, it was unlocked, but now that it is your portal, you lock it when your first session is completed and need to unlock it next time you use it, and lock it again when finished. With your black mirror made, you have the necessary tool for the companion quest in the next chapter.

chapter

6

Entering Otherworld

I find it mildly troubling that there is a tendency for some people to aspire to be fairies, elves, or some type of Other People. This is reminiscent of the kind of debilitating energy found in the fairy tales of people dying from longing after being in contact with the Fair Folk. You need to keep in mind that they are they and you are you. It can be that when people become so involved with maintaining a daily alt-identity with other beings—be these elves, fairies, vampires, werewolves, dragons, unicorns, and so on, even going so far as to have medical procedures done to enhance the role they have embraced—that they are losing track of their own identity. The dressing up and taking on a persona can be fun, but if it becomes the norm, then this can become problematic and might indicate personal issues with self-esteem or past traumas that have not been resolved by a thorough chakra clearing.

By being mindful of the difference between you and them, you do not insult the Other People, and you do not denigrate your own being. Witches tend to be more comfortable in their own being and can work with and consult with the varieties of people in Otherworld, with spirits, and with the deities without trying to BE them. Maintaining your own spiritual identity will allow you to move from life to life without becoming lost or confused.

What you do after this lifetime is for you to decide later, but it is important to understand that adopting a persona can form a blockage to having an actual experience. If you are too busy being the elf, you may prevent yourself from meeting elves. What you might think of as complimentary may indicate to the Other People that you lack the necessary grounding for successful contact. You may also be setting up restrictions in your own mind as to how the Other People should look, sound, and behave. How would you feel if someone started imitating you, yet ascribed attitudes to you that you don't actually have? There is a distinction between fantasy and accessing an alternate dimensional reality.

Seeking an Otherworld Companion

There is a ritual for contacting the Other People that I call the companion quest, but this should only be conducted when you are fully prepared to follow the Otherworld rule that you must be a good friend to gain a good friend. This means that you don't get to lay out parameters of who or what your companion will be. Another important rule to keep in mind prior to entering the quest is that what you take into Otherworld is what you will find there, so you need to be grounded and in a good frame of mind, with a heart-set of love and a mind-set of trust.

Some years back I regularly conducted open circle esbat rituals for both full moons and dark moons. The term "open circle" means that anyone can attend, no matter what their spiritual path—no membership required. These days I limit myself to open circle sabbats, and fortunately a local coven has been helping me out by presenting two of the sabbats annually. With each full moon esbat and dark moon esbat that I led, the circle was cast and a ritual was held that included an appropriate magical project, and it was brought to a close with refreshments, followed by a benediction and opening of the circle. At one dark moon esbat that was the second dark moon in the same solar month, called the Sidhe (or Fairy) Moon, I conducted a companion quest for those who were interested in meeting someone from Otherworld with the possibility of gaining an Otherworld friend.

In attendance at this particular esbat was a person who came out of respectful curiosity but was settled in an Eastern spiritual path. I explained about the quest to everyone in the circle and said that only those who were interested in making contact with someone from the Otherworld should come, one at a time, to sit in front of the black mirror after I opened the portal. Several chose to sit, including the curious individual, while the rest simply stood by in the circle. Afterward, I asked if anyone cared to share their experience with the group, and two did. One person only felt intense heat in front of the mirror and decided that the time was not right for contact, but the person who attended to explore another spiritual path actually had an encounter.

There is a distinction between fantasy and accessing an alternate dimensional reality.

The surprised participant saw the forest and path I had described, and while sitting in front of the mirror, looking in, saw a centaur walk out of the woods onto the road, pause, and look out at the person. When asked if he was to be a companion, the centaur casually responded, "No, I just came to see what's going on," and continued on across the road and disappeared into the forest. I have to admit, I've never seen a centaur in Otherworld (so far), and knowing that someone else had really made my day! This also shows that the Other People are *aware* when a portal is opened.

At a different sidhe moon esbat and companion quest, everyone in the circle came one at a time to sit at the mirror, and in this event each person had an encounter. After the ritual ended, some participants were able to quickly find a portal stone to utilize as their personal gateway for further communication with their new friend. At another time, a person told me about once having a connection that was lost and now desired to reconnect with the Other People, so I offered some suggestions. By following my advice and directions, the person was surprised to discover the Other People had just been waiting for the invitation! It is always a delight to me when someone returns to let me know they've had a successful encounter, or reunion, and feel they are on a fulfilling path. The information I am presenting here is what I have been doing for those who want to make this kind of meeting. If you are uncertain, wait until you feel more ready.

Sidhe Moon Esbat and Companion Quest Preparation

I prefer to only insert the companion quest ritual during the second dark moon in the same solar month as part of the sidhe moon esbat, which is a relatively rare event; however, any dark moon could be appropriate as long as a Faerie circle is cast with the appropriate changes shown for this below. The quest is inserted in the place usual for magical works during the esbat, but this will require some initial work in the kitchen and taking it to the circle area or setting up a means for brewing tea within the circle. I have used a Mrs. Tea set (with a teapot and a brewing machine) for myself or for small groups. With large groups I have used a 60-cup coffee brewing canister to make hot water, then added the water to one or two large teapots when the time arrived in the ritual. I put the herbs within the teapot and used a hand-held strainer when pouring the fairy tea into the teacups. For one sidhe moon esbat and companion quest, I used a number of sets of demitasse espresso cups and saucers, which worked out perfectly.

You only need a little tea, but if you enjoy it (as most people do), you can pour yourself and your Otherworld guest a full teacup. Read through this section before attempting the ritual, making sure you have everything you need in place when ready to begin the ritual.

Preparing the Companion Quest Circle

The altar should be a table placed at the west of your circle and covered with a cloth. You will not need altar candles, images for the Lady and the Lord, or a pentacle, for you will be having tea for two. You will need:

- your athame and wand
- incense
- prepared blessed water made with burdock root
- the covered black mirror at the center of the table
- a gray or white short (votive) candle in a container in front of the mirror
- 2 taller gray or white candles (pillars or tapers) flanking the mirror
- a small bowl of rose petals and a small bowl of milk placed forward of the mirror and flanking it with one bowl at either side
- a container with a bit of mugwort (to add to the votive candle)
- the tea things (see below)

Set one chair at the table behind the mirror so it is at the west for the companion and is facing east. Have another chair for yourself facing the mirror and the opposite chair (so you will sit facing the mirror, and behind that, facing you, is the companion's chair). Have a place on the altar for a teapot with a hot pad or a warmer underneath, a tea strainer and small saucer for it (if none in the teapot), and have two cups with saucers and two teaspoons. If you use a sweetener and/or milk, you will offer these to the companion as well, so only have a small amount of each in containers, as the remnants will be poured on the ground after the ritual. Have a plate with two shortbread or other type of tea cookies (found in the cookie section of most grocery stores).

Prepare yourself for ritual in your usual manner. When ready to begin the ritual, boil a kettle of water. Pour a little hot water into the teapot to warm it and pour that out, then, with a set of measuring spoons, prepare a pot of fairy tea, taking your time as you say the words while dropping the ingredients into the pot:

(3 TEASPOONS BLACK TEA)
Black for power,

(½ TEASPOON CHAMOMILE)
Apple of night,

(1 TEASPOON DANDELION ROOT)
Root of the sun,

(½ TEASPOON ELDERFLOWER)
Lady's blessing,

(1½ TEASPOONS HOPS)
Lord's leap for joy,

(½ TEASPOON MUGWORT)
Then between the worlds,

(½ TEASPOON RASPBERRY LEAF)
to Fairy bramble,

(1½ TEASPOONS ROSE HIPS)
With token of love,

(ADD THE BOILING WATER)
Brewed to bring Fair Ones close to me.

Cover the teapot with a folded tea towel or a tea cozy to steep and stay warm.

Casting the Sidhe Moon Esbat
and Companion Quest Circle

Sweep the circle space deosil starting at the west, with the table and chairs inside the circle:

> *As I sweep may this space be cleared of any negativity*
> *and chaotic energies so that it is made ready for my work.*

Light the incense:

> *I am about to cast the circle wherein I may greet the*
> *Other People and seek the blessing of the Goddess and the*
> *God in their aspects of Queen and King of Otherworld.*

Light the gray votive candle and take it to the quarters widdershins (west to south, east, north, and back to west and the table):

> *I call upon the light between the Waters*
> *to illuminate and protect this circle.*

> *I call upon the light between the Fires*
> *to illuminate and protect this circle.*

> *I call upon the light between the Airs*
> *to illuminate and protect this circle.*

> *I call upon the light between the Earths*
> *to illuminate and protect this circle.*

Set the candle in front of the covered black mirror.
Raise your athame at the altar:

> *The circle is about to be cast in the presence of*
> *the Lady and Lord of Otherworld, to be a place*
> *where the Other People may manifest and bless*
> *me, who am their friend in this world.*

Point the blade at the west as you cast the circle deosil (west to north, east, south, and back to west):

This circle is cast around me, above me, below
me—as a sphere is the circle cast and consecrated
so that only love may enter and leave.

Sprinkle blessed water around the circle widdershins, then fan the incense around the circle widdershins.

With your wand, call the elementals deosil starting at the west:

I call upon you, elemental Water, to attend this
rite and guard this circle, for as I have fluids
and emotions, I am your kith and kin.

Continue to the north (Earth/body and strength), east (Air/breath and thought), south (Fire/vitality and heat), and return to the altar table.

Draw above the table the symbol for infinity, the cosmic lemniscate (sideways 8), with your wand:

Hail to the elementals at the four quarters! Welcome,
Lady and Lord of Otherworld! I stand between the worlds
with your love and power all around me, and I call upon
you to bless my communion with the Other People.

Set the wand down. With the athame, bless the hot, steaming teapot:

I bless this tea as a union of Water, Fire, Air, and Earth,
through which I honor the power and grace, beauty
and strength of the Lady and Lord of Otherworld.

Set down the athame and greet the Other People with open arms:

Hail to the People of the Land of Mist! I send my
greetings and ask that you hear my call and let the
gateway be opened between us in this world and
Otherworld. In the names of the Lady and the Lord
do I call upon the Fair Ones in peace and love.

Remove the cover from the black mirror.

Pull out the chair behind the mirror to offer it to a companion:

> *Here is the place at the table*
> *made ready for my guest.*

Return to your side of the table and lift the gray working candle above the altar:

> *As the light shines brightly before me,*
> *let the light of Otherworld reach into this place.*

Set the candle in front of the mirror and add a little mugwort to the flame:

> *Mugwort to increase psychic energy and*
> *power so I may easily connect with those*
> *who will aid me in my companion quest!*

With the forefinger of your power hand, draw the sign of the pentagram at the lower right of the mirror, then sweep your hand across the front of the mirror as though opening a door or sweeping aside a curtain, going from right to left.

Light the candles at the sides of the mirror and sit in your chair facing the mirror:

> *Here lies the doorway into Otherworld.*
> *I welcome my guest through this portal.*
> *May those Other People who choose to visit find*
> *this gateway and be revealed as my guest pleases.*

Gaze into the mirror and envision a misty, fog-shrouded Otherworld forest. Feel the cool, refreshing air, smell the damp leaves and the moss on ancient trees. Hear the sound of water rippling along a narrow winding brook and the delicate, soft, hesitant footfalls of a browsing deer rustling the fallen leaves. Listen for the quiet steps of your guest approaching through the dark forest, coming toward you. The forest will remain in view behind the guest so that the table will appear partly in wood-land, with the sounds of forest animals and the brook continuing in the background.

You will recognize the guest has arrived when your feel a "presence," hear a subtle voice, or see something happen in the mirror. The compan-ion may appear as a light, a blur, or an image, or you may attract other visitors. Speak in your mind to the guest who comes to you, remember-ing to be polite and use good manners, taking care with your words, and if you make a mistake, acknowledge that and ask pardon.

When you feel someone has arrived, you may stand up to lift the bowls of rose petals and milk, one in each hand, to greet your guest:

> *Hail to thee and blessed be thy feet that brought you on*
> *this path, blessed be thy heart that beats steadfast, blessed*
> *be thy eyes that see between the worlds, blessed be thy*
> *hands offered in friendship and accepted in true friendship.*

Set down the bowls to flank the guest's tea setting behind the mirror, and over the top of the mirror offer both your hands together, palms up, fingers bent toward the palms[6]:

> *I am honored by your presence, and you are*
> *welcome at this table set between the worlds.*

Release the handclasp and sit again. In your mind introduce yourself by your Craft name (or mundane first name or usual nickname if you have no Craft name):

> *I greet you most heartily. I am called _____.*
> *How may I call you that we may commune*
> *with one another in the bonds of friendship?*

---

6   The guest lays hands palms down onto your palms-up hands, with fingers of both hands hooked together. The handclasp would be like if you held your right hand palm-up and your left hand palm-down in front of yourself and gripped the fingers; each thumb would be on the outside of the opposite hand's little finger.

Pause and listen. If you hear a name in your mind:

> *I am pleased that you have come, and I invite you*
> *to sit with me so that I may serve you tea.*

If you do not hear a name, the person may have simply been curious or not ready to say a name, but you will give the Other the opportunity to stay or depart:

> *I am pleased that you have come, and I invite you*
> *to sit with me so that I may serve you tea. If this is*
> *not to your pleasure, then I will give you my blessing*
> *to take with you as you take your leave of me.*

If you feel the guest is staying, you may now serve tea to the place set for the guest, standing and resuming your seat as necessary. Pour some tea through the strainer and into the cup, set a cookie on the saucer, then sit at your place and pour some tea into your cup, set a cookie on the saucer, add sugar and/or milk as desired, and offer the sugar and milk to the guest by setting the containers close to the guest's cup and saucer.

Bless the meal:

> *I know of my needs and offer my appreciation to*
> *that which sustains me. May I ever remember the*
> *blessings of my Lady and my Lord of Otherworld.*
> *The Lord brings spiritual life through the bounty*
> *of the Lady so that all is created in undying*
> *beauty. I honor the inner beauty of the spirit.*

Eat and drink with your guest, visiting and discussing through thought your desire for a companion. If you and your guest feel compatible, you both may decide that the guest is to be your companion. You can then ask for aid in finding a crystal that will be suitable as a portal you can carry as the gateway for your companion.

When finished, stand:

> *I am blessed by your having shared this tea with me.*
> *My blessing I give to thee, for we have come together*
> *in friendship and depart in friendship. Merry we meet,*
> *merry we part, and merry we will meet again.*

See the guest stand, extend your hands together, palms up, feel the cool touch of the guest's hands in farewell, and release.

Sit again and look through the candle flame into the mirror. See the misty forest becoming darker as you hear the quiet footfalls of the departing guest disappearing into the wild wood. The splashing of water in the narrow brook becomes fainter, the deer bounds off into the depths of the wood, the forest fades away and disappears, and the door between the worlds gently closes. You see now only the black mirror and your reflection.

Take a deep breath, hold a moment, and release, feeling yourself becoming more aware of your surroundings. Take another deep breath, hold a moment, and release, feeling yourself returning to normal awareness. Take a third deep breath, hold a moment, and release, feeling yourself aware and refreshed.

Raise the votive candle:

> *Let the gateway between this world*
> *and Otherworld close once more*
> *as I take my leave of the Other People*
> *in peace and love. So mote it be.*

Set the candle down, snuff it, and gently sweep your power hand across the front of the mirror going left to right, as though closing a door or moving a curtain back, and draw with your forefinger the pentagram at the lower right corner of the mirror as you whisper into the mirror:

> *The gateway is closed and sealed.*

Cover the mirror.

Opening the Sidhe Moon Esbat
and Companion Quest Circle

With hands open over the table:

> *Lady and Lord of Otherworld, Fair Ones of the*
> *Land Beyond, I am blessed by your sharing this time*
> *with me. Watch over and guard me; guide me here*
> *and on all my paths. I came in love and I depart in*
> *love. I honor the Lady and the Lord of Otherworld,*
> *where the spirit is nourished in song and joy.*

Raise the athame upright:

> *Love is the law and love is the bond.*
> *Merry meet, merry part, and merry*
> *meet again. So mote it be.*

With hands open over the table:

> *Beings and powers of the visible and invisible,*
> *depart in peace! You aid in my work, whisper in*
> *my mind, bless me from all realms and worlds you*
> *inhabit, and there is harmony between us. My*
> *blessings take with you. The circle is cleared.*

Farewell the elementals at their quarters, moving around the circle widdershins (west, south, east, north, and back to west):

> *Depart in peace, elemental (Water, Fire, Air, Earth),*
> *my blessings take with you. Hail and farewell!*

Take the incense and smudge deosil (clockwise) around the circle from the west:

> *This space is purified by the smoke of incense*
> *so that all energies, spirits, and entities return*
> *to their realms with my blessings.*

Sprinkle blessed water around the circle deosil from the west:

> *This space is cleansed by the blessed water and the*
> *gateways are closed and sealed. The circle is cleared.*

With the athame, open the circle widdershins (west, south, east, north, and back to west):

> *The circle is open, yet the circle remains*
> *as the magical power is drawn back*
> *into me. The circle is cleared.*

Touch the flat of the blade to your forehead to return the energy inward, then touch your palms to the earth or floor as an aid for grounding and bringing yourself back into balance on this plane.

Returning to This World

Remember that an unprepared visit or being overly interactive with the Other People can lead to debilitating illness, listlessness, and depression if you are not cognizant of possible disruption to your nervous system and cellular structure. Like staying in the sun too long, you can find yourself spiritually dehydrated. The tendency to jump into something new with huge enthusiasm can cause you to throw caution to the wind, so it is important to stay grounded. The food and drink served is not consumed by the guest, but its essence is removed, so do not eat or drink the guest's portion. Release the remains (tea in the cup and the cookie on the saucer) to Nature by taking these outside and pouring and crumbling them onto the ground.

After the ritual, you will probably need something more to eat and drink, even if it is only a cookie and some juice. This is also a good time to write about your experience in your journal, not that you will forget, but this activity helps to ground excess energy and bring you fully back into this world. If this first encounter yielded no connection, give it another try another time.

Using a Black Mirror

The black mirror you create can be used as any scrying tool as well as a portal. It can be used for divination and for travel to Otherworld, dimensional travel, contacting guides, and viewing past and future events. After a little experience, you will find your own uses for the mirror; let the mirror be your inspiration. I prefer a mirror that is at least 5×7 or more in size, although a smaller, palm-sized one is good to carry for relaxed meditation. The larger mirror works best when set on a table while you sit in a chair facing it.

Seeing Your Past Lives

Place a short unlit candle in front of the covered mirror and candle snuffer, lighter, or matches to one side. For this ritual, I prefer a white votive candle in a votive holder, but black or purple is also a good choice. While you can do this in a bright room, I personally prefer to have a dimly lit space for mirror gazing prior to casting the circle. Cast your circle, then sit at the table and take a few deep breaths, feeling cleansing energy when you inhale and increasing relaxation when you exhale each time as you release tension from the muscles in your body and then return to normal breathing.

When feeling relaxed and centered, uncover the mirror, unlock and open the portal as described earlier, and announce your intention:

With this mirror do I see my past lives.

Light the candle and gaze into the mirror, seeing your reflection in the dark glass:

Show me my past lives.

Look past the candle flame at your image, blinking as needed, and you should see your features start to change. You may see yourself in a past life as male or female; some people have even seen themselves as animals. The idea of transmigration of souls is part of the Hindu belief in regards to reincarnation, so seeing an animal looking back at you could be an indication that there is a basis for this theory. It might also be that an animal spirit guide is looking through the portal to gaze at you. Trust your intuition in determining this based on the impression you got when you saw the image.

When you see your own face return to the mirror, it is time for you to end the session. Depending on what you saw, you may learn more about your past lives with subsequent viewings or you may discover your past incarnations were elsewhere or in other forms. I know of people who have seen themselves as neither human nor animal, but as a different being altogether, lending credence to the idea of starseed people incarnating on Earth.

Take and release three deep breaths to return to normal awareness. Raise the votive candle:

Let the gateway be closed. So mote it be.

Snuff the candle. Close and seal the door:

The gateway is closed and sealed.

Cover the mirror.

Seeing Ancestors

When looking for images of your ancestors, remember that these are the people from whom your body descends. Your past lives were in other forms, not necessarily related to the body you currently reside within. Each body has its own mitochondrial and genetic heritage. You selected this heritage prior to incarnation for a reason that may not be clear to you now, but seeing your ancestors may give you some insight to the purpose of this incarnation or to aspects of your life that have puzzled you. The realization of the symbiotic relationship of body and spirit is why the body is referred to as a person's temple in many religious traditions. The ancestors you see may have influenced your body shape, your sensitivities, your physical attributes and your mental aptitude, and emotional attitudes. You can specify if you want to focus on maternal or paternal lineage, or just see who shows up. You can narrow your focus by asking what this incarnation, in this tapestry of ancestors and genetic heritage, comes through as an influence in who you are today.

When you are ready, place the unlit votive candle in front of the covered mirror, with matches and candle snuffer to one side. Cast your circle, then sit at the table and take a few deep breaths, feeling cleansing energy when you inhale and increasing relaxation when you exhale each time as you release tension from the muscles in your body and then return to normal breathing.

When feeling relaxed and centered, uncover the mirror, unlock and open the portal as described earlier, and announce your intention:

With this mirror do I see my ancestors.

Light the candle and gaze into the mirror, seeing your reflection in the dark glass:

Ancestors of my body, kin of my blood,
show me your faces so that I may sense
what imprint of you I carry in me.

Look past the candle flame at your image, blinking as needed, and you should see your features start to change. When an image appears, ask in thought what you have inherited from this person. The personality of an ancestor may be buried deep within you or it may be more overt. You might discover that you have embraced positive qualities that came from one and worked to counter negative qualities that came from another. You may find there are strengths that you can draw upon in times of crisis or need, or there are qualities that are repressed or manifested that you can now acknowledge, seeing yourself as a symbiosis of genetically influenced body and Universal Spirit of Light.

When finished, take and release three deep breaths to return to normal awareness. Raise the votive candle:

Let the gateway be closed. So mote it be.

Snuff the candle. Close and seal the door in the usual manner:

The gateway is closed and sealed.

Cover the mirror.

Ancestor work can be very enlightening and give you insights to your own habits and characteristics, be these physical, mental, or emotional. With this knowledge, you can ask the ancestors to help you overcome the negative and enhance the positive for your personal self-improvement, focusing on the merits and purpose of this life for personal growth and inner peace. With new awareness, you may feel more able to focus on the talents you chose to obtain and experience in this life, and you may have better communication with your body, understanding the interconnection of body and spirit working together.

Gaining Information

To get answers, learn things, or see present or future events, the mirror can be used. For this type of scrying, I prefer a small mirror, made with an oval 4-inch photo frame so I can sit with the mirror resting in the palm of my hand. You can make both sizes of mirrors at the same time. The black mirror effect for scrying can also be created by using polished black obsidian or a scrying bowl that has a dark surface and is filled with water.

Have your intention or reason for scrying stated as you begin so you won't just see random disconnected images. By focusing on a question or what you seek to see, you can gaze into the reflective surface until visions appear. When you see what looks like clouds are passing in it, stay relaxed as images relating to your intention are now likely to start appearing. It is okay to blink when scrying, no matter what tool you are using, be it a crystal ball, black mirror, palm stone, or your morning coffee.

Meditation Portals

Meditation can be used for expanding your own awareness and to spread out into your surroundings, but the process of meditating can also create a portal to contact the Other People and the Divine to receive answers to questions, gain insights, and elevate your own spiritual development. Meditations can be recorded and then played back, but I prefer to simply follow the process in my head so I am not restricted to someone else's tempo or imagery, or even my own since I prefer spontaneity.

I once sat with a group on a guided meditation to the English Isle of Apples (Arthurian Avalon), and all was going well in the meditation as in the astral we gathered near a lake. I could even see some of the other participants in this journey. At one point we were led to embark on a boat to reach the isle, and the meditation guide referred to the person steering us across the lake as the ferryman. I and one other partici-pant in this astral vision looked at the tall, slen-der, shimmering, fair male and shook our heads apologetically, for we recognized him as a noble elf and not the traditional Greek ferryman who takes the dead to Hades's Underworld. He sighed, then laughed and said, "No, I am not Charon, and this is not the River Styx." We both laughed with him, and when we arrived on the isle, the meditation guide took us to stand-ing stones and continued from there. When the guide directed us back to the boat for the return trip across the lake, the tall elf smiled at me and the one other person who had recognized the inconsistency in terms earlier. He motioned us over to stand near him, which we did, and we had an enjoyable passage back. Of the group, it appeared that only two of us had felt the incongruous imagery in the meditation.

If you follow the meditation process in your head, you can follow your own tempo and be spontaneous.

Afterwards, just to confirm to myself that we really had been on this astral journey together, I quietly asked the other person if anything unusual had transpired during the meditation, and this resulted in the entire process being recounted to me the same as I had seen and experienced, including the words spoken by the elf that made us laugh, and thus we both had validation that we had indeed travelled together and had seen other members of the group as well. A good meditation can take your spirit to another world or dimension, so when creating your own meditations, it is important to keep things in proper alignment, although in this case, it was pleasant for both of us to have a special interaction with a gracious elf lord.

Creating Your Sacred Meditation Space

By not setting a theme or program for your meditative travels, you let things happen and you know that you are not experiencing a consciously pre-planned event. There is an easy technique for getting into a meditative state, and you should practice to create a comfortable sacred space in the astral realm from which to launch into your journey. The astral plane is a kind of region not located in Otherworld nor this world that acts as an in-between launching site.

Setting up the meditation process can be done without words. You simply get into a relaxed position, preferably sitting in a comfortable chair or on a cushion on the floor. I do not recommend lying down as that might put you to sleep, and the purpose of meditation is not sleep but travel. The relaxed state allows you to remain alert while thinking your way through the steps of creating and later accessing your sacred space. From there you can access the Akashic Records; make contact with the Divine, ascended masters, spirit guides, or meet with people from (or within) other dimensions, including Otherworld; or go on a journey of exploration for inspiration and insight for problem-solving.

You can enter meditation without any accoutrements or you can light a candle and incense if that helps set the tone for you. I do not recommend background music if that becomes the focus for you, as you will be doing your own entry and exit from the meditation. To create your sacred space (or temple) for meditation, state your intention prior to beginning with something like:

I will create my sacred meditation space.

Keeping your eyes mostly closed, but not completely, focus on taking three deep breaths, with the intent of using the exhales to remove any stress, worries, or extraneous thoughts from your mind. Next, begin to relax your muscles from the top of your head through your face, your neck, your shoulders, your upper arms, your lower arms, your wrists, your hands, your fingers, your torso, your upper legs, your lower legs, your ankles, your feet, and your toes.

Envision a slow counting of numbers starting at ten and going down to one, seeing each number in your mind's eye, perhaps as drawn on a chalkboard, with each number being wiped away and replaced with the next until you get to one. The appearance of the numbers may change as you go along or remain in the same style or theme. Now visualize the chalkboard becoming transparent, turning gossamer with a slit down the center through which you see a gigantic tree close behind it. You walk through the slit and go to the tree, which has an immense trunk, large roots, huge branches, and a height that disappears into the sky above. You see that its wide-spreading branches show the four seasons—with the left side bare branches with snow for winter, then colorful leaves next to that for autumn, budding new leaves for spring, and green leaves to the right of that for summer—so now you know that you are standing before the world tree. This tree is a universal image, be it the tree of life, knowledge, or the world, with branches for all the seasons or focused on one season. This is your visualization, so let yourself see what is most comfortable or meaningful for you.

Now visualize that as you look at the huge tree and its giant roots, you spot a large heavy-set carved or otherwise decorated door under an arcing giant root, through which you can enter. Whether it is a door or an opening, this entry is meant just for you. By passing through this portal or opening the door, you come to a set of stairs going down into the earth below the tree. Now you will slowly count down again with each step, from ten to one, and upon reaching the bottom of the stairs, you find another door. This second door is closed and you know that it belongs only to you. Notice how it appears; if you like, you can change it. Only you have the ability to open the door, and when you do, you enter into your personal sacred space, where you can begin to envision what it looks like. It can be a temple, a courtyard, a grassy plain, a forest bower or spring-fed pool, a stone fortress, a comfortable sitting room, farmyard, stable, or anything else that appeals to you.

Each time you enter your sacred meditation space, you can decorate it as you like.

Each time you enter this space, you can decorate it as you like, adding to the scenery, making changes, or bringing new objects into your space. It is from this place that you will depart on your journeys. You may find your power animal or your spirit guide awaiting you. Before you leave your sacred space to go on any journey, look around and see if there are trails, river channels with perhaps an awaiting boat, and so forth, then set your intention as to what question you desire answered, which trail you would like to explore, or simply use the meditation time to work on the appearance of your temple. From here, your sacred space, on each journey you will discover new pathways to explore to find answers to your questions and encounter just the right people to help you find solutions to problems.

When your meditative journey is completed, come back to normal awareness by returning to your temple from wherever you have traveled. Depart your sacred space by closing the door behind you, going back up the steps and slowly counting from one to ten, leaving through the doorway in the roots of the tree, walking back to the gossamer chalkboard and on through it, turning around to be where you are seated or laying down, then slowly counting from one to ten as you wiggle your toes, flex your ankles, move your legs, then your torso, arms, wrists, fingers, neck, and head. You know that when you reach the count of ten, you are fully alert and back in normal awareness.

Meditation for Seeking an Answer

State the purpose for your journey, then take yourself into the meditative state as previously shown. When you reach your sacred space, you will see a new pathway leading away from your sanctuary. Your spirit guide or power animal may be waiting there to accompany you. Move from your sanctuary to the path, and notice all the details between the start of the path and your sacred space. There may be a field with tall grasses or one filled with flowers, such as with a field of lavender. You are comfortable and secure, knowing that you are taking a journey to find the answer to your question.

At the path now, you see it leads into a woodland, and you proceed into the cool dimness of the forest on the dirt path. As you walk along the path with confidence, you gaze into the forest now and then to see if you can spot a deer or other animal. Your guide is at your side now, and you walk together close to a rippling brook. The clear water splashes over rocks in the stream and you wonder where the source is. You can barely catch a glimpse of tall, rugged mountains through the dense foliage of the forest, but you know you are not travelling that far.

Now you see a large pond of clear fresh water surrounded by ferns and slender trees. Nearby is a large boulder, and your guide motions you to the stone, where you climb up for a better view into the water. As you look into the water, you see a large trout swimming lazily along the bottom. Now you recognize where you are, for this is the pool surrounded by nine hazel trees, and the ancient trout eats the hazelnuts of wisdom that fall into the water. He is the guardian at the entry to Otherworld, filled with the knowledge of the ages. You ask the trout if he will answer your question. The fish swims to the surface and you are not surprised when he speaks, "State your question." You do this, and he dives back to the bottom, eats a hazelnut, and swims back to the surface, breaking through with a leap and returning with a splash before sticking his head out of the water and speaking to you. Listen to what he says. Remember what the trout tells you. The trout flips back into the depths of his pool with a splash and disappears into the darkness among the stones.

Your guide now shows you back to the forest path. Together you walk back to the edge of the forest where you entered, and your guide returns within as you continue back to your sanctuary. From your sanctuary, you now return to the door, closing it behind you as you go back up the steps and follow the route back to normal awareness. Each time you visit your sacred space, your temple or sanctuary, you will find new paths to new areas where you will receive guidance and knowledge, contacts, and new inner awareness in a safe and secure environment. You may create other sacred space in this world or discover new entrances to your temple, rather like having a main house in one area and a vacation cabin in another. You can plan which place you will go to prior to your meditation or you can let yourself be surprised.

Other locations that may appear on different paths might include a cave near the top of a mountain where you can encounter the Crone stirring her cauldron, within which you may see visions in a swirl of mist, hear whispered answers in a boiling brew, or see visions in rising steam. You might find two paths leading up to the cave; one your guide tells you is an easy but unremarkable walk, while the other is harder but more scenic, and you decide which path you will take. Sometimes you might find that you are starting out at the cave with a panoramic view below, and you can simply enjoy the view or decide where you will wander once you have your bearings. The world of your meditation grows and widens the more you utilize it, and you may find new wonders with every visit, places and connections that offer assistance to you. A waterway may develop in your sanctuary with a comfortable boat moored for you to travel on, gently taking you to other regions of your world. The possibilities are endless and not necessarily earthbound, but open to the Universe and to other dimensions when you are ready to visit. Your guide may be an animal spirit guide, an ascended master, spirit guide, or Otherworld companion, but they are always someone you can trust, for you will have the heart-set and mind-set of Perfect Love and Perfect Trust.

Calling Upon Spirits, Ascended Masters, and Deities

When you have opened the way for communication and contact, you can address anyone and anything for answers and guidance in any matter. To a witch of the Old Religion, the Goddess and the God are a reality, as are spirits, guides, and ascended masters, so communication can be as casual as ordinary conversation. You talk to the Goddess and the God, to the elementals, to the Other People, to your spirit animal guide, to the entities and spirits of Nature, and you *know* they understand and will respond. Be respectful and sincere, and you will receive an answer. I use the expression "call upon" rather like when someone calls upon a friend, knocking at the door, saying, "I was in the area and thought I would drop by. Do you have a moment to visit?" You are not invoking or commanding, banishing or discharging: you are courteous.

Simply speak aloud your question or need and see who answers.

It is possible to direct your communication to someone in particular, but I have found it more spiritually rewarding to simply speak aloud my question or need and see who answers. That way I anticipate the matter will be addressed by whoever has the greater knowledge, ability, or interest—a spirit guide may respond by sending you a telepathic message, a sudden insight, or through automatic writing; a deity may come as a vision; one of the Other People may leave something meaningful and direct you to it through an empathic pull; the elementals may respond with an action related to the elements. With automatic writing you may find that the question or problem spontaneously occurs to you, and by writing that down, the response follows.

Sometimes questions arise that are triggered by incidents, something read, or comments from other people, and you can simply take a moment of quiet time and ask aloud for insight. At a gathering, someone mentioned the "dark night of the soul," which is when a person goes through such a period of deep anguish as to feel isolated from the Divine. That night I wondered aloud what could make me feel so despondent, and the Crone suddenly appeared and gave me the answer, which was something I had not previously considered. My reaction was to reaffirm my trust in her, and that made all the difference. I saw the Crone with new eyes, as it were, and know she will always be there for anyone who turns to her for comfort in rough or unhappy times. We can speak to the invisible world as we would to people around us and receive a reply, so we are never alone, nor are we ever isolated.

We can speak to animals, and from the heart, they will hear and understand. That doesn't mean they haven't got their own issues and concerns, only that you can become cognizant of these and work with them, not against them. In my experience, some animals, such as cats and dogs, are more likely to communicate in telepathic images. I saw my cat intently looking at the step through the bottom of the screen door, and I asked, "What are you looking at?" and mentally saw a terra-cotta flower pot on the step with a coiled-up black snake inside it. When I went to look, there the pot was on the step, complete with a black garden snake. By opening up the channels of communication, these branch out into more and more directions, bringing greater awareness and connection with this world and other worlds and dimensions. All you need to do is ask.

Contact can also be made with tools such as the black mirror, crystal ball, runes, tarot cards, and so on. Open the conversation:

I call upon the Divine, the Universe, ascended
masters, spirit guides, animal guides, and helpful spirits
to aid me so I may have a meaningful reading.

Then ask your question or state your concern and work with the tool of choice to receive the answer, knowing that you will not be let down. In doing readings, you may receive an impression of a spirit's presence, see a vision, hear a voice, or gain an unexpected insight. You can prepare yourself for the experience by creating your own little ritual prior to beginning your work with a tool. The tool is only that—an aid to opening the portal through which someone will speak to you in a manner you can comprehend or will learn to comprehend. Your ritual could be as simple as lighting a candle and a stick of incense or as complex as you desire, with casting a circle and calling the quarters and the Divine. Above all, there is heart-set and mind-set.

Crystal/Gemstone Skull Portals

Crystal skulls can be made of quartz crystal, citrine, topaz, aquamarine, amethyst, or fluorite, but the skulls may also be made from other mineral gemstones such as any of the varieties of jasper, carnelian, tiger iron, hematite, blue stone, jade, and more. Not everyone resonates energetically to skulls or the stones they are made from, so it can be a matter of trial and error or of touching or holding the skull to determine if it feels right or extends an energy to which you are receptive. Skulls can be used as a focal point for meditation or they can function as a doorway to other dimensions, usually through the eye sockets, forehead, or crown. I usually see these skulls as portals to other worlds, dimensions, astral plains, and more, but also as conduits to beings such as ascended masters, spirit guides, deities, Otherworld, and possibly even to people in other regions of the galaxy.

Take the time to sit quietly, looking at the skull, and if you have a question, ask it in your mind and wait for the reply. When you hear the response, acknowledge it and accept it. Perhaps you will need to reflect on the reply for a while to understand the deeper meaning or perhaps you will know exactly what you are being told. If you don't trust the messenger, you are not likely to follow the message, so if crystal skulls are an uncomfortable venue, use something else. A person's individual response to or connection with the portal is what makes it a viable tool. After you work with a crystal, gemstone, or mineral skull a few times, you can create a gateway that brings those you are consulting closer to you.

I was never a "skull person" until I encountered a pair of life-size skulls of golden topaz identified as a male and a female by their shaman caretaker, with the female smaller and the male larger, but each projecting a distinct energy. These skulls came from the Chinese mountain range of Bayan Har, north of Lhasa, Tibet, in the region of the Dropa people, and they changed my understanding of crystal skulls. Although skulls have been considered a conduit for communication with the ancestors, spirits, and deities, many people consider skulls scary and threatening. My initial perspective was one of curiosity and a bit of skepticism, but I gave focusing on them a try. First I sat in front of the male to receive a message and said aloud, "I brought a notepad to write down any message." Instantly I heard, "Put it away; you won't forget what I tell you." That was a *wow!* moment that took my breath away for a second, and with utter delight I dropped pen and pad to sit happily with the skull.

I heard the voices of both the female and the male; after the first private session with them, and for months after their caretaker took them home, they appeared as spirit apparitions to answer questions and give advice. Once the connection had been made, it became ongoing. Over time I learned that there were others who sat with the skulls and experienced the same phenomenon: after first contact, the two have easy access and will come and help with questions and offer advice. I have been privileged to have them at the shop several times, including for a group meditation when the earth aligned with the galactic center in 2012. During one visit the female instantly healed a physical problem for me when I sat with her, and at another time she appeared in full form as a female figure wearing a simple white long-sleeve robe and standing beside me to offer encouragement during an energy training class.

At a different private session with the skulls, I heard only one word from the female and it concisely distilled my concern. When I sat in front of the male, he spoke to me and showed me an amazing vision that reinforced what she had said. In a part of that vision, I saw him in full form, attired as she had been when I saw her in class. Over the years I have accumulated a number of skulls since the first session in 2010. I select them by the empathic energy emanating from the skulls, some for healing, some for grounding, some for communication, and some for the connection between them and the skulls I originally encountered. I bought an apple-sized crystal skull for their first visit, which I set in front of the female to be "energized," and I was astonished to see a quick bolt of light dart from her eye sockets directly into those of my crystal skull. The person standing next to me glanced at me and asked, "Did you just see that?" I confirmed that I had, and we both had validation that we saw the same thing.

Crystal skulls can be a portal to another dimension or to another part of the galaxy or universe.

Skulls can be a type of portal to another dimension or to another part of the galaxy or the universe. After visiting with the two skulls off and on over the years, I believe either case could be right. When looking for your own

personal gemstone skull, let the energy you pick up from a skull tell you if it is right for you. One skull I liked was simply too high energy for me but was perfect for someone else much younger. Sometimes a skull will indicate it wants to be with you, but after a time you understand that it now needs to move on to someone else. If you have misgivings, don't try to force yourself to embrace something that bothers you. You won't hurt their feelings. But if you feel comfortable, relax and let the skulls speak to you. Just as an example of this, I once was concerned that a skull I had placed on the table without a cushion might prefer to have one, so I said aloud, "Should I put a cushion under you?" and I laughed when I heard the reply: "I'm a stone. This is fine." The point is, these **ARE** stones, but they are also *portals* through which beings in other dimensions and worlds can make contact with us. The energy of stones varies with their constitution, but crystals record and transmit, as do other stones, such as granite. Jade is considered a good luck stone because of the traditional understanding of its positive energy emissions, and jaspers are generally protective or have healing qualities.

Dream Portals

Another way to converse with the Universe and enter into Otherworld is through dreams. When you are perplexed about something or need information or counseling, at bedtime simply ask the Universe to give you some advice, then put the matter out of your mind and go to sleep. In ancient Greece there were dream temples for people to do this very thing, with a group of priests and priestesses who in the morning would interpret the dreams of the temple guests. With "lucid dreams" the common description is that the dreamers know they are dreaming and may be able to manipulate events in the dream, but this does not take into account the actual meaning of the word *lucid* as distinct and quickly understood communication, and so I include dreams that offer an awareness or insight that may have been previously obscured or unknown. Such dreams are usually spontaneous but can be preprogrammed for gaining information and having a genuine experience that may involve dimensional travel by simply stating a question to the Universe at bedtime. In one case, this brought me both a horse and a poem describing my dream, which I had to jot down quickly as it literally sang through my mind.[7]

I had been with a group of Pagans who were at one point in the general conversation talking about the Ted Andrews book *Animal Speak*[8] wherein he talks about finding your own personal totem animal, also identified as a spirit animal, animal guide, or power animal, whose energy you learn to work with. Although the book states clearly that such animals come to you and are not chosen by you, most of the participants discussed which

7   See "The Wild Mares" in *Grimoire for the Green Witch*.
8   Pages 7–19.

animals they had selected as their totem animals and why. I didn't have one because I was unable to pick a favorite from among the wonderful creatures of the earth. Over the years I have received messages from hawk, vulture, deer, squirrel, cat, dog, cardinal, blue jay, butterfly, and ant, to name just a few, so there was no one animal I could name as my totem.

Simply voicing a desire can send a message to the deities or the Universe, so a few days later I sat on the edge of my bed at night and said, "I like so many animals; which one is my totem?" I put the matter out of my thoughts and went to sleep and had a dream filled with beautiful music as I stood at twilight in a misty rainfall amid richly green grassy hills with a cliffside dropping off to the ocean at one side. The quotes in the poem were my spontaneous dream words, and to be honest, I had never before called on the horse goddess Epona: "Epona, Epona, send me the wild mares!" She answered by sending a herd of white mares over a hill to me. One mare from her herd stopped for me and chose to be my spirit animal guide, and I rode off with the herd on the mare's back, and she has been with me ever since as a guide.

Once you have a power animal, it will appear in meditations or symbolically in the same type of animal you encounter in this world, so pay attention to the meaning you associate with that animal and any message you may be receiving. I was taught that white is the color of fairy horses, and as a child, whenever we were out driving in the car, my mother used to tell me to make a wish when I saw a white horse, lick my right forefinger, and clap it on my left palm to stamp it, like posting a letter to Otherworld for fulfillment. Fairy horses can also be black, but they tend to be more rambunctious and unpredictable, and are generally associated with the Wild Hunt.

The night that I asked for a "totem" animal, I received in my dream a white horse from a herd of mares with tangled manes sleek with rain, and I assumed the mare was just that—a mare. My horse accompanied me on meditative journeys and showed up in lucid dreams. During one meditation, however, I was walking alongside the mare on a path in the woods when I mentally voiced a question, and to my surprise, the mare answered. Only then did I realize my spirit horse was a friendly pooka! I asked why she hadn't talked before, and her practical answer was that until now, I hadn't asked her anything. In my power animal dream, I was longing to go where the Other Folk had gone, and my last words in the dream were: "Epona! Epona! You heard my call to thee! You sent me wild mares to ride across the Elder Sea!" So, while I assumed the horse that I had ridden in the herd was a fairy horse and able to take me to Otherworld, I thought she was like other fairy animals, such as fairy cattle, rather than a pooka. She was quite amused, and now we chat more often.

You can receive answers through dreams for any question you ask, even mundane ones.

By making a request to the Universe prior to sleep, you are contacting the Divine, who will appear in whatever form they choose for manifestation, and thus you can receive answers through dreams for any question you ask, even those you may feel are mundane. I was once approached by someone who was habitually unkind but now claimed a desire to make amends, so I asked the Universe if this person was sincere and could be trusted. That night I dreamt I saw a large black rabbit reclining like a person would in a rocking chair on the porch of a plain wood cabin with a door and one window. I stood nearby next to an elderly woman wrapped in a blanket who spoke to me and said, "I am Grandmother Osen. Listen to what Grandfather Hare has to say." In my dream I walked over to the porch and up the steps to stand near the hare, who said, "Kiss me." When I leaned forward to follow his direction, I saw his large, sharp teeth and I drew back. The rabbit said, "That is right. The wild things *stay* wild." Within that dream those words reminded me that I had once before accepted the person's offer to make amends, only to have the unpleasant behavior repeated later on, and I knew that this time would be no different. I had my answer. I told the hare that I appreciated the insight and asked if I could hug him.

He said yes, so I did and then returned to Grandmother Osen, and we exchanged a hug, and then it was as though I stepped out of the scene through a doorway and woke up.

I later searched to see if there was a meaning for the dream name and came across *oscine* (os·cine/os'cen[9]), and from there I found that *oscen* ("oh-sin"), which was the name as I heard it, is Latin for "songbird" and was believed to foretell the future by its call. Although there may perhaps be no connection, Grandmother Songbird seems appropriate for both the wise Crone figure in my dream and the purpose I had set before the dream.

Dream portals can be used to find things, enter Otherworld, contact ascended masters and spirit guides, and solve problems. The portal is opened when you quietly address the Universe, the Divine, and initiate the conversation just prior to going to bed. Put the matter out of your thoughts, get under the covers, and go to sleep. You could have a pen and paper nearby so when you awaken you can jot down a few notes about what you learned, but I have found the images are so distinct they simply do not fade away even after decades have passed. But if you start hearing a song or a poem, start writing at once before it fades away. When I was a child my mother would interpret my dreams, teaching me the nuances, reverses of some images, and how some elements related to awake-time events or questions, but she always insisted that I eat something first to remain grounded in this world while recounting the energy from the dreamscape.

When you ask your question or seek advice, have the matter you are going to address already formulated in your mind so you can be concise. Limit the scope of the issue so you are not rambling and looking for a pack of divergent bits of information but for something distinct that can be answered quickly and concisely. The dream portal is activated once you fall asleep, and it may be that your subconscious mind has tackled the problem, gotten some input from the Universe or Akashic Records,

---

9   https://www.merriam-webster.com/dictionary/oscine

and then presents the solution or answer to you as a parable, poem, or short story, or it can be that you actually have an encounter through your subconscious mind or a dimensional portal with beings from another place. The response may not come the first night you ask but may simmer along for a few days until you are no longer so focused on getting the answer, then it pops into your head or comes as a powerful dream. Once the dream has arrived, you have the response, and the portal closes. Try not to overwork the portal, for not every question needs to be addressed to the Universe, although you will probably feel instinctively which question will receive an answer. It is a matter of speaking your request from the heart.

Scrying Through Nature Portals

There are many varieties of portals that can be accessed in Nature. Some may occur spontaneously as you are mulling over a matter, and others may come into being and depart after delivering the needed message or vision. While these visions may be dismissed by others as examples of pareidolia, in which a person finds patterns or images in random things, be it clouds, a crystal ball, or the milk in your morning coffee, witches call it *scrying*. I once stirred the creamer in my coffee and for a test, I said aloud, "Show me something that I will recognize today." In my cup the creamer formed into an inverted rose on a long stem, then faded into the coffee. Later that day I visited a store where the clerk had pinned a rose upside down on the wall to dry it out. This was simply an experiment on my part to prove to myself that you can scry anything.

There are so many things that can be used for seeing past, present, future, people, places, events, and more that it is unnecessary to give them all labels. The more you scry, interpreting the things around you as you feel drawn to do, the greater the ease in making the connection for communication with the Divine, the Other People, spirits, entities, and ascended masters.

Visions in Clouds, Water, Smoke, Leaves, and Flocks

Clouds can be a terrific portal for seeing what is coming or receiving messages from Spirit, the Universe, the Other People, guides, and ascended masters. When you are in alignment with the energies around you, the clouds become a source of communication. When people see the Wild Hunt, they are within roiling black clouds moving with ferocity across the sky. When I saw black unicorns rampaging across the sky, they were in a churning mass of black clouds, but upon calling on the white unicorns to steer these away from habitations, a mass of puffy white clouds arrived with a herd that pushed the black clouds away. There may be occasions when images are giving you answers, confirmation, or information, so do not dismiss the images you see in the clouds. Just because you see fierce energies in the clouds does not mean there is no remedy, for you can also call upon the elementals to take those out to sea, for example.

Smoke's color, form, and the direction in which it moves can be clues for communication.

When driving a long distance to the hospital to see my mother one last time before she passed, I saw white smoke rising in great plumes into the sky from a roadside burn while I worried that I would not make it in time. Suddenly the smoke turned black, and the Crone was clearly visible as a hideous hag looking down at me. In a crackly voice, she said, "I am going for your mother, but I will wait for you." I knew then that the physician's assessment of my mother's condition was accurate, but I replied in thought: "I'm not afraid, for I know you are also the Mother." Instantly the cloud turned white again, and the most beautiful image of the Goddess smiled down at me and spoke in a gentle voice, "Only those who do not know me fear me." She immediately vanished and there was only smoke in the sky, and I was able to have one last memorable time with my mother.

After her passing, she dropped in now and then, and even let me know she was there to greet my brother when he passed away in his sleep just a few years after her.

People will scry campfires, bonfires, and more, looking for information, seeking an answer to a question, or even greeting an elemental entity. Smoke has been used for divination throughout human history, probably since the first campfire. It is used in religious ceremonies and rituals worldwide as a portal to the Divine, a conduit for communication.

Everything from the color of the smoke, its form, and the direction in which it moves can be clues for communication. The dance of the flames or smoldering of hot embers in a fire can also reveal images, elemental spirits you can address. When addressed, the fire and smoke may afford you insights or even show images of future events that allow for making changes and directing energy to modify or otherwise use.

Being open to communication will allow conversation to flow in many forms.

By scrying anything, you not only receive information, but you can act on it and turn the energy if necessary. Positive affirmations, lighting a candle with an intent stated, carrying an appropriate stone, etc., are just a few of the methods for moving energy. There may be times when a flock of birds flying in the sky gives you an insight or when you look into a rain puddle or still water that you see something meaningful. The portals are more accessible when you live in awareness that being open to communication will allow conversation to flow in many forms, give warnings, open opportunities, and provide information that can be beneficially utilized.

Repetitious Sightings

Besides the usual type of scrying, you may be given symbolic conversation. Seeing the same animal or bird in your daily activity, when this is not the norm for you, indicates a message. If you keep coming across the same image in different manners, pay attention and research the meaning associated with the image. If, for example, you see a blue jay flying by, then later on see a picture of a blue jay, and then see a piece of jewelry featuring a blue jay, this is definitely a message. Blue jays are alert, intelligent birds that noisily set up the alarm for other creatures when a predator is nearby, and they are also mischievous and curious. You may want to pay more attention to your surroundings, your interactions with others, and perhaps even call upon your spirit guides and the Divine to watch over you as you go about your day.

Repeated sightings of a hawk may indicate the need to stay alert, especially if you are driving or doing any activity with the potential for distraction. I once saw a hawk flying by as I was driving my car, then another hawk in a tree as I passed by, and finally a third hawk as I drove up an on-ramp to an interstate highway, and I felt the need to slow down. When I rounded a blind curve in the ramp, there was a large piece of metal on the road that I was able to navigate around without incident. Had I not slowed down, the matter would have gone differently.

Repetitious sightings include animals, birds, insects, and any object that you recognize as unusual in seeing multiple times and gives you the sensation of a message being given. Not all such sightings are warnings, for many times there are messages of reassurance and well-being. Finding a dime in the parking lot, then finding a penny on the lawn, then finding a quarter in your pocket when none should be there tells you that things are looking up and there is positive energy around you that you can direct for success in any area you choose; just say: "Let this influx of positive energy bring me the promotion I seek," or whatever it is that you desire. Sometimes the repetition is a reminder of what you are trying to achieve or what you are trying to avoid. Just being alert to what others might consider random coincidences will open a portal that brings you a sublime connection with the flow of the Universe.

Retaining an Ongoing Relationship
with the Other People

Once you have opened a portal to Otherworld, you will find that synchronicities occur more often and that the nature of the communication may vary, sometimes coming in a spontaneous vision or through ritual, meditation, or dreams, and sometimes through encounters with people who have a different aura about them that lets you know they are "Other." To maintain a good relationship with the Other People, you need to be respectful and nonjudgmental. We are not the measure of all, and indeed we often know less than we think we know. An attitude of openness and a heart-set of love combined with a mind-set of respect and acceptance will draw the Otherworld and its many different inhabitants closer to you.

Treating your contact experiences as a matter of course and avoiding the reaction of suspicion or fear will go a long way to keeping the contact open. The more you learn about those you encounter, the more they learn about you.

The heart-set of Perfect Love and the mind-set of Perfect Trust will see you through the portals.

That is balance. If you are not willing to accept this, then perhaps you are not ready for Otherworld contact. Your trust in the Divine should be the light that shows you the way into other dimensions and worlds.

When working with the Fair Folk, be they elves, dragons, unicorns, or sprites, you need to be aware of the meaning of your words and nuances of communication. I have mentioned substituting "desire" for "want," but you may discover that there are many such words with meanings that may need to be clarified. The art of dialectics is more than simply using logical speech to examine ideas; it includes knowing how words can be understood. If you find yourself in a verbal stumble, acknowledge your error, for we all make mistakes in our word choices at one time or another, and try expressing your thoughts in a different way. If you have blundered into a situation that becomes too constrained, back out graciously, admitting that you feel you are perhaps a bit out of your depth. Part of learning is experiencing mishaps that you can admit to and putting that knowledge to work to avoid further pitfalls.

By setting out a beverage for, or in honor of, the Other People during the full moon, by meditating or scrying during a dark moon, by creating sacred space to honor the Other People, by pacing your realm, by seeking a companion, and by talking to invisible spirits and to animals, stones, and all else around you, you are setting up the framework for opening the portal to an expanded awareness of the multidimensional, multiverse, and transdimensional reality in which we actually exist. The heart-set of Perfect Love and the mind-set of Perfect Trust will see you through the portals.

Afterword

Connecting with the Other People involves establishing a special relationship that must be approached with care and thoughtfulness. It is my hope that you will find my instructions and examples useful and informative, and possibly use these as a way to create personal, safe, and rewarding encounters—but only if this is a lifestyle that you truly desire. I do not by any means want you, the reader, to use my experiences as a gauge for your own, for each of us is a unique individual. Instead, let the instances you read serve as illustrations of possible scenarios and a sample of some of the types of wonders that are out there, waiting for you to extend an invitation for connection and communication.

Until you actually have an Otherworld encounter, it is difficult to substitute incredulity with knowing, but after such an experience, you may find that you feel a bit out of sync with the so-called normal world until you are able to find your balance between this world and your interaction with the liminal. By opening portals to Otherworld and making contact with the inhabitants, you straddle both sides of the threshold. But rest assured, once contact is made, whole new worlds will open up to you, other beings will greet you in friendship, and people who have had similar experiences will be drawn to you or you will be drawn to them. The gateway to Otherworld, other dimensions, and planes of existence awaits those who seek it. If you choose to embark on this adventure, then blessed be the feet that walk the Otherworld path, the heart-set of empathy and love that attract new friendships, the eyes that see between the worlds, and the mind-set that receives knowledge and communion with the Divine in all worlds and dimensions.

Bibliography

Andrews, Ted. *Animal-Speak: The Spiritual & Magical Powers of Creatures Great & Small*. St. Paul: Llewellyn Publications, 1993.

Briggs, Katharine. *An Encyclopedia of Fairies: Hobgoblins, Brownies, Bogies, and Other Supernatural Creatures*. New York: Pantheon Books, 1976.

Evans-Wentz, W. Y. *The Fairy Faith in Celtic Countries*. Secaucus, NJ: Citadel Press, Carol Publishing Group Edition, 1994.

Moura, Ann. *Green Witchcraft: Folk Magic, Fairy Lore & Herb Craft*. St. Paul: Llewellyn Publications, 1996.

———. *Green Witchcraft II: Balancing Light & Shadow*. St. Paul: Llewellyn Publications, 1999.

———. *Grimoire for the Green Witch: A Complete Book of Shadows*. St. Paul: Llewellyn Publications, 2003.

Sams, Jamie. *The 13 Original Clan Mothers: Your Sacred Path to Discovering the Gifts, Talents, and Abilities of the Feminine Through the Ancient Teachings of the Sisterhood*. New York: HarperCollins Publishers, 1994.

Simmons, Robert. *The Pocket Book of Stones: Who They Are & What They Teach*. Berkeley, CA: North Atlantic Books, 2015.

Index